REN VAND

Richard
1 Corintheans 2 : 9

Ren Vanderton

9/28/18

GOD'S
PLAN

ELIMINATE BIBLICAL IGNORANCE

REN VANDESTEEG

GOD'S PLAN

ELIMINATE BIBLICAL IGNORANCE

Published by Redemption Press, PO Box 427, Enumclaw, WA 98022

Toll Free (844) 2REDEEM (273-3336)

Redemption Press is honored to present this title in partnership with the author. The views expressed or implied in this work are those of the author. Redemption Press provides our imprint seal representing design excellence, creative content, and high quality production.

I intentionally refer to the devil in the lower case, rather than honor his names with capital letters.

I give a scripture at the beginning of each chapter that supports the chronology and topic of that chapter.

ISBN 13: 978-1-68314-399-4 (Paperback)
978-1-68314-400-7 (ePub)
978-1-68314-401-4 (Mobi)

Library of Congress Catalog Card Number:

Table of Contents

CHAPTER 1

Problem: Does Anyone Read the Bible Anymore?

"My people are destroyed from lack of knowledge [about God]."
(Hosea 4:6 NIV)

GOD WANTS PEOPLE TO know Him. He does not want humans to live in ignorance or be destroyed from lack of knowledge about Him. He is within our reach. Think of it! We can tap into the celestial mind of the universe and receive His help anytime, anywhere. He communicates His thoughts to us. He makes Himself available to us.

Most people think the Bible is a "good book." Some read it. Yet there is a huge gap between God and people. In the United States only one in ten apply God's teachings to their lives.[1]

We all have problems throughout life and need help. The Creator-God, who knows everything, wants to help us in our problems. We find that help in the Bible.

The Bible says, "[God] . . . planted eternity in the human heart . . ." (Ecclesiastes 3:11) Eternity, in this case, means God put an impulse into humans. This impulse motivates us to reach beyond our lives toward God.[2] We learn about Him in the Bible's central message. Read it and soak it in.

Understanding that message is an easy and thrilling trip through God's book. "And this is the way to . . . know . . . God . . ." (John 17:3)

Light splashed on the old, brick church. It glowed against the backdrop of clouds and coming darkness. The sun hung like a huge orange fireball against the deepening blue sky. The brick walls warmly welcomed me as I parked my car. It was a Tuesday evening and I was eager to teach a class of godly people who had left the drug culture. I felt exhilarated.

As I opened my car door, the leftover heat from the 102-degree day hit me like a furnace blast. I walked around to the side door of the church. That is where I heard Ray's boom box serenade the street. All the way from the basement, the lyrics to the song *Victory in Jesus* were clear and loud. As I walked down the dimly lit stairs, I gingerly made my way down as my hand squeezed the rough railing.

In the classroom, some students silently read their Bibles while others sang along with the lyrics. Ginny, a girl who lived on the streets, swayed and danced to the music. A rough, accented voice broke through the din.

"Hey, Pastor Ren!"

"Hi, Don. How you doing?"

"Great!"

Another voice joined in, "Chaplain, can I show ya this a minute? It's great!" Moe yelled from across the room.

I walked to the other side of the room to see why he was so excited. His face glowed and he smiled from ear to ear as he showed me a picture of his ex-wife. He was dating her again, hoping they would remarry. While I looked at her picture, Moe leaned into me and with a serious tone in his voice, said, "She loves me, man! She told me so."

"Success to you, Moe! Jesus knows her heart and yours. Let's make it work this time."

"Thanks Pastor, we will."

After a few high-five greetings and slaps on the shoulder, I made it to the front of the room. I laid my binder and Bible on the clear, plastic podium. I was ready to teach. That is when Gary approached me. He looked troubled. With an exasperated, stuttering voice, he seethed, "The Bible is . . . so . . . so . . . complicated. I like some of the stories, don't get me wrong, but it's a tough read, man. I know it's supposed to help me but I can't make it work for me. When I did drugs I got high, ya know what I mean? I'm free from 'em now because I know Jesus . . . but I can't make heads or tails about this book. Ya know what I mean?"

His eyes pleaded and I heard the cry of his heart: *Can you help me?*

Gary, an ex-convict in his fifties, served twenty-three years in prison for drugs and aggravated assault. A few years earlier, God set him free from the steel grip of drugs. When he won his freedom, Gary started the next phase of his life. Now, he is walking with God and growing in his relationship with the Almighty. He is a diamond-in-the-rough in God's jeweled tapestry.

Randy, on the other hand, was an executive in the entertainment industry. I met him at a different church. He had a perfectly trimmed beard, and wore a silver suit with a blue silk shirt, striped tie, and alligator shoes—top-of-the-line. Looking good was important to him. He also had a desire to know and understand the Bible and God. With this in mind, he decided to buy a Bible. He told me later that he thumbed through Bible after Bible in a Christian bookstore. Finally, he gave up in exasperation. "I can't make sense out of these Bibles. I want some freedom from my problems and these Bibles aren't showing me how to get it. What's the use?" He slammed the last Bible shut, crammed it back into its box, and banged it back onto the shelf, not caring if anyone saw or heard him. He fumbled for his keys, stomped toward the exit, and with his head down, punched through the door and bolted out of the store in disgust.

Gary and Randy are two men from diverse backgrounds who believe in the same God. One is a fifty-something former drug addict; the other is a successful filmmaker, well-known and respected in his church and community. In addition to having Jesus in their hearts, they had something else in common—a desire to understand the Bible. They thought that if they understood it they would know how to get help from God for their problems.

They were good men; however, they were unsure how to use the very book that has the answers to their problems. Gary knew a few stories in the Bible, but rarely cracked it open for himself. It was the same with Randy. These men exemplify one of the problems in our modern era; namely, most people do not know how to read the Bible, so they rarely pick it up at all.

That was me in my youth. I grew up in a Christian family but did not learn how to read the Bible. In fact, I did not bother with it unless I had to in church, Sunday School, or Catechism class. Someone gave me a Bible as a graduation gift when I finished high school. Once home, I put it in my bedroom closet, way in the back on the top shelf, closed the door, and promptly forgot about it. Some people buy a Bible and lay it on a coffee table where it looks good. I put mine in a closet. That was a sad chapter in my life. I look back with regret on the years when I did not understand God's book or how to use it. I know I was not alone.

There are many reasons people do not dive deep into the Bible—but the result is the same: alienation from God followed by a life filled with disappointments. I did not understand God or the freedom He offers. That ignorance imprisoned me. I lived for entertainment, parties, and "the good life," while I ignored God and His Word. I empathized with Gary and Randy because I had felt the same frustration.

One of many reasons people lack knowledge of God and the Bible is the teaching of secularism. The goal of secularism is to create a god-less or secular society and to influence church members to ignore God and the Bible. This philosophy subtly creeps into culture and rejects public displays of Christian faith and worship.

This belief system crept into European culture for many years and now boldly and publicly fights Christian faith in the United States. For example, prayer was taken out of American public schools in the early nineteen sixties. Now public prayer is frowned upon. If there is prayer, it better not end in Jesus' name. Many people are not allowed to display their Bibles in the workplace.

In this twenty-first century, our language has subtly changed from "freedom of religion" to "freedom of worship." The first phrase represents the belief that a person is free to believe and practice his or her religion privately *and publicly*. The second phrase represents the secular belief that people are free to worship within the walls of a church, but not in public or at work. Atheism and our modern culture are kissing cousins to secularism.

Could it be that the Bible is the most non-read bestseller ever? According to Charisma Magazine, " . . . it is still the most popular book ever. The Bible ranks at the top of favorite book lists among Americans. It is also the best-selling and most widely distributed book in the world. Nearly four billion copies of the Bible were printed and sold globally in the last five decades – far exceeding any other book."[3]

Os Guinness (PhD, retired professor, Oxford, England) put it this way, " . . . soft preaching, diminished book reading, online information, over-busy lives . . . general shallowness . . . Evangelicals . . . are no longer distinguished for their deep and faithful knowledge of the Scriptures."[4]

Secularism imposes a life on people that pushes God to the side. Consequently, we often have little time left for Him. Secularism perpetuates an attitude against anything that smacks of faith or religious jargon.

For example, "Don't bring repentance into our conversation. I don't like religious words and I'll end this conversation if I have to."

Due to secularism, some people ignore God. They disregard the life-building teaching in His Word and go on their way. They think they are free. In reality, they are like flies stuck in a sticky flycatcher, unable to free themselves from ignoring God. Others are too busy to read the Bible because they are focused on making money and getting ahead in life.

These situations have reached such proportions in Western society that sometimes folks cannot even find a Bible to buy.

"'May I see your Bibles, please?' a man asked while in the book department of a major store. Under 'Religion' he found books on Yoga, Buddhism, Islam, and even witchcraft. But the Holy Bible?

'No,' he was told. We don't stock Bibles.'"[5]

Did the store deliberately ignore the Bible by not stocking it? Whether they did or not, the result is that the Bible was not available. That may be enough to discourage some who look to the Bible for answers.

Not reading God's book of answers creates a spiritual vacuum. That opens us up for secular humanism. We may easily slip into a spiritual black hole and grow further away from God.

Many people believe that since they do not read the Bible they cannot expect to know much about it. However, they may erroneously think it is no big deal. They just join the crowd and make the most out of life without it.

That may work for a while. However, they may not be able to explain why they begin to feel empty and unfulfilled over time. They may think, "What is life all about? Why are we here?" Not all of life is doom and gloom, but they have a gut feeling that something is not right. The more they struggle to free themselves from their problems, the more they seem to sink into a suffocating hole.

Those who experience these feelings may become philanthropic. They try to please people, be kind, humanitarian, civic-minded, patriotic, and helpful to others. They give time, money, and gifts. They want to be liked and noticed. They strive to have their egos stroked. They may be driven to attain an education, to excel in life, and to make a difference. In the process, they may nod toward God, but still have the feeling that something is wrong.

To better understand this dynamic, let's summarize the secularizing process, which causes a two-part problem:

1. Many people lack biblical knowledge.
2. Due to this lack of knowledge they do not know God and live imprisoned lives.

They do not know how God can set them free from whomever or whatever captivates them. Porn, drugs, wrong self-esteem, broken relationships, and unbelief in God are a few examples. They will continue to live imprisoned lives until they discover how God *can* and *wants* to set them free.

Secularism is only one of many reasons why people lack knowledge of the Bible. Another reason is that many do not realize the Bible is a library of books. The word "Bible," derived from French, literally means "library." The Bible is a collection of sixty-six books written by approximately forty men over a period of roughly two thousand years. The Bible is confusing to many because they do not know how to read this collection of books.

Together we will learn what ties everything together in the Bible. God has given us the critical component that unlocks the meaning to His Word. That component is what we will discover in this book.

I am a retired pastor and military chaplain, ordained by the Christian Reformed Church. I pastored for five years and served thirty-one years in the U.S. military; six as an enlisted airman in the U.S. Air Force and twenty-five as a chaplain in the army and air force.

When I served as a chaplain I lived in the U.S. and Okinawa, Japan with my wife Carol, and sons, Mike and Dan. After Mike and Dan left for college, Carol and I had various assignments in the U.S. and two in Europe. In addition to these assignments, the air force deployed me to the Middle East to serve in the first Iraq War (Operation Desert Storm) in 1990 – 1991, and the Bosnian War in Europe in 1997. I retired from active duty in 2004 in San Antonio, Texas. I served as an associate pastor at Oak Hills Church and Air Force Village Retirement Community (now named Blue Skies of Texas). I am no longer on a pastoral staff. However, I continue to preach, teach, consult with churches and various organizations, and mentor pastors, chaplains, and others throughout the San Antonio area.

I preached, led Bible studies and coached life groups in Asia, the Middle East, Europe, and the U.S. One theme permeated all these places: while most people were ignorant of the Bible, many wanted to understand it. That was true for Okinawans, Japanese, Koreans, Arabians, Eastern Europeans, Western Europeans, and Americans. This led me to believe that biblical ignorance is epidemic within the organized church and pandemic throughout the world.

We do not need to live in biblical ignorance. God has the solution for our Bible-less, God-less, imprisoned, over-busy, secular lives. He has placed eternity in our hearts and wants to set us free from our lack of knowledge and imprisonment. The classic Christian hymn, *Faith of Our Fathers* captures this truth in its second verse.

"And through the truth that comes from God,

Mankind shall then be truly free."[6]

The purpose of this book is to know God. We will accomplish that by eliminating biblical ignorance.

CHAPTER 2

The Solution to Biblical Ignorance

" . . . the Spirit teaches you everything you need to know . . ."
(1 John 2:27)

PEOPLE WANT A GOOD life. They want to be happy, have their needs met, be healthy, live in abundance and in peace. God also desires those things for us. If our desires match His, we can attain those goals according to His will, especially spiritually at the deepest level in our lives.

The Bible has one central message with one main character—Jesus.

That's it. That is the Bible in a nutshell. Simply trace its one central message and if you believe it, you will know God. God sets us free as we learn and accept the meaning of that message. Jesus gave a hint toward that when He said, " . . . you will know the truth, and the truth will set you free." (John 8:32)

Biblegateway.com did research conducted on 250,000 people in churches. They studied fifty factors that impact spiritual growth. Their findings?

"Nothing has a greater impact on spiritual growth than reflection on Scripture . . . If churches could do only one thing to help people . . . they would . . . equip their people to read the Bible . . . for meaning in their lives . . . The Bible is the most powerful catalyst for spiritual growth. The Bible's power to advance spiritual growth is unrivalled by anything else we've discovered."[7]

By learning the Bible's central message, we discover that humans need God and He has a plan for how He helps us. Imagine watching God paint a picture of a landscape. On the canvas, He paints the sky, then adds the sun. Next come some clouds, land and mountains, and a tree trunk, followed by a branch. After that, a few leaves and some animals. The artist continues until we see the entire landscape.

In an analogous manner, we will see the progression of how God reveals Himself and develops His plan in the central message of the Bible. That message runs through all sixty-six books of the Bible. When I learned that one central message, the Bible made more sense to me. The stories, events, people, locations, dates, authors, and even the maps, fit into a symmetry I had not seen earlier.

That message can be compared to the central nervous system in the human body. The spinal cord begins at our brain stem and runs down through our vertebrae to our tailbone. Along the way, nerves branch off from the spinal cord into our arms, abdomen, and legs, reaching all parts of our bodies. Similarly, the Bible's message runs throughout the book and branches off to other stories, people, events, prophecies, and teachings.

God's Word is written mostly from His point of view. Learning this reference point enables us to quickly understand our need for Him. God met our need for Him when He sent Jesus to our world approximately two thousand one hundred years ago. Many people don't even know they have a need for God. That shows how severe the human situation is. But God knows our situation and He has the solution. That solution is "[Jesus] gave his life to purchase freedom for everyone." (1 Timothy 2:6). Let's unpack this signature verse.

When Jesus came to our world He exposed the heart of our passionate God. He wants to unite with us in a perfect relationship. He never stops loving us, even when we live in willful disharmony against Him. God wants us to live in right relationship with Him. If we align with God, He sets us free.

You may ask, "Free from what?" or "What is freedom?"

When we experience the freedom God gives us, we live liberated lives. While we live in that freedom we obtain God's help to our problems—whatever they are.

Let's start the process of receiving God's freedom with a true-life example. Did you ever buy something that you had to assemble, such as a bike or a piece of furniture? Did you ever try to put it together without reading the instructions? I have. Once I bought a bookcase with five movable shelves. I dutifully unpacked the crate, laid out the parts, and began to put it together. I thought I could figure out how to put it together as I went along. "Who needs instructions anyway?" However, my non-mechanical brain did not understand how to put the lousy thing together. Meanwhile my wife, Carol, waited patiently with instructions in hand. When I reached the boiling point of total frustration and was ready to give up, she gently reminded me that assembly instructions came with the kit and offered to read them to me. Sheepishly I gave in and followed instructions as she read them. I was surprised how quickly it all came together. Lesson learned.

Many people do something similar when it comes to their attempt to build a life without reading the Bible. How many of us have faith and want to build a life in God but do not read His instructions? Our lives can be like that bookcase with parts scattered on the floor. Instead of bookshelves and screws, we have money, jobs, families, sports, cars, friends, schools, diets, and rest, laying in pieces on the floor of our lives.

The parts are there but they are not in their proper places, nor are they functioning as needed for a well-oiled life. Many of us may honestly try to put ourselves together without God's help. When we try, we do not learn what He teaches and we end up living in disarray; we will call the disarray *prison*. Lack of biblical knowledge leads to bondage.

Do you know what God thinks about our not knowing His Word? Don't worry! It's not bad news. He told us that He " . . . overlooked people's ignorance . . . but now he commands everyone everywhere to repent . . . and turn to him." (Acts 17:30)

God does not want us to disregard Him. He is willing to overlook our lack of knowledge if we turn to Him. That means to change from doing things our own way. Repentance literally means "to change one's mind." We change our minds about living apart from God. Once we decide we want to understand Him and His book, God will meet us in our desire and set us free. Jesus said He came to give us an abundant life. (John 10:10) The more we turn to Him, the greater we comprehend God and what life is all about. As we seek relationship with the Almighty, intimacy grows and we begin to experience His freedom.

Remember the people I wrote about earlier, those who God called out of the drug world? They used to be street people, drug addicts, pushers, convicts, prostitutes, and pimps. These believers in Jesus now enjoy life; they praise and thank God for setting them free from drugs. They are an example for all humanity. God can set us free from anything that enslaves us.

Let's join them and other believers around the world as God leads us to His freedom by using the following acronym: A R I.

A = *Action*: We search for and discover the Bible's central message.

R = *Result*: We believe that message.

I = *Impact*: We know God and He sets us free.

We will start our trip to freedom where the Bible starts—at the beginning.

CHAPTER 3

Creation: The Greatest Show on Earth

"In the beginning God created the heavens and the earth."
(Genesis 1:1)

WHEN YOU READ A book where do you start? At the beginning, of course. It is the same with the Bible. When you open a Bible, does it start with something big or something bad? It starts in Genesis chapter 1 with Creation—something big. Many people treat the book as if it started with sin—something bad. However, sin did not show up until the third chapter in Genesis.

Many people are told that because they are sinners, they need God's salvation. For this reason, they go to the Bible to find an answer to the sin; or look for help to endure a problem. Consequently, many dive in and start to read wherever they think they can find an answer or help to their predicament. Their desire may be wonderful, but they shortchange themselves by taking a shortcut around Creation. They bypass the first few chapters and start at Genesis 3 instead of Genesis 1. Starting this way leads to confusion; starting where the Bible starts leads to clear understanding.

The following humorous example is an object lesson for how not to use the Bible.

A man wanted to know God's will about a particular problem. Knowing the Bible is a holy book, He thought God would guide Him if he randomly opened the book, put his finger on a verse, and then did whatever that verse said. With this in mind, he opened the Bible and without looking, put his finger on the verse, "Judas betrayed Jesus."

He thought, *I don't want to do that. I'll try again.*

He closed the Bible and then opened it again. This time he put his finger on the verse, "And Judas went out and hanged himself."

Well, that's not good either, he thought. *I'll try one more time.*

Again, he closed and opened the book. This time his finger pointed to the verse, "And what thou do'est, do quickly!"

Many people come to God's book, take a verse out of context, and try to apply it to themselves. They find out that does not work. God wants us to understand His book correctly, and the way we do that is to start at the beginning.

Without Creation, we would not properly understand that God intends to restore humans to the original state of freedom He gave Adam and Eve when He created them. If we begin at the beginning, we will understand that God planned to redeem humans because it was His desire that we live eternally in the freedom that He originally gave at Creation.

Did you ever make something out of nothing? Neither have I. Only God can do that. Even in our creativity, we use materials that already exist. Our heavenly Father can do anything, including make something out of nothing.

The Hebrew verb *bara* means "to create out of nothing." The verb *asah* means "to make something out of something else." God does the former, we do the latter. Artists can create a beautiful painting but only by use of canvas, paints, and brushes that are already made from other materials. Look long and hard at the *Mona Lisa* or the *Night Watch*. They are beautiful and priceless paintings—but they have been made from materials already in existence. Not so with God! He created His awesome universe and perfect people from nothing.

Not only did God create the universe out of nothing, His qualities of eternal power and divine nature have always been seen in His creation. This is one of the reasons God created the universe. He wants His creatures, we humans, to see Him in His creation. The sight makes us worship Him because He is so majestic. The whole purpose of the human race is to worship God. He gave us that truth when He said, " . . . for I have made them for my glory." (Isaiah 43:7) When we give glory to God, we worship Him. This is part of the biblical story. "For ever since the world was created, people have seen the earth and sky. Through everything God made, they can clearly see his invisible qualities—his eternal power and divine nature." (Romans 1:20)

God made it easy for us to know Him:

Look up
- See the sky
- The sun
- The moon
- The stars
- The clouds
- The rain

Look around
- See the earth
- The mountains
- Canyons
- The rivers
- The oceans
- The fish

- The plains
- The wheat
- The crops
- The animals
- The birds
- The trees
- The flowers
- The people

When we look at God's creation we see His divine nature, His love toward us, and His eternal power. Worship!

To keep His creation perfect, God told Adam that he may freely eat the fruit of every tree in the Garden of Eden except for the tree of knowledge of good and evil. God followed that with, "If you eat its fruit, you are sure to die." (Genesis 2:16-17) Everything is perfect but God brings one picky, little detail to Adam's attention. "Don't eat from this *one* tree."

Imagine the scene: Adam and Eve had hundreds, maybe thousands of trees from which they could eat. Imagine your favorite peach, apricot, pomegranate, almond, walnut, cherry, mango, or orange tree. They could choose any of them or a myriad of others to satisfy their appetites at any time. God gave Adam and Eve this abundant life of freedom to enjoy to the fullest.

The Bible started with something big, really big—God's perfect creation. That perfection included the *crème de la crème* of life, namely, freedom with God. This was His plan for us from the beginning. Just as He personally related to Adam and Eve in the Garden of Eden, He desires to relate with us in the same way. Just as He walked and talked with them in the cool of the day, He wants to walk and talk with us. He is totally free and wants us completely free.

But something dreadful happened . . .

CHAPTER 4

Fall: Thud
The Devil Imprisons People

"But the Scriptures declare that we are all prisoners of sin, so we receive God's promise of freedom only by believing in Jesus Christ." (Galatians 3:22)

ADAM AND EVE HAD the good life. They enjoyed themselves, were infatuated with each other, loved life, took in breathtaking nature, dined on scrumptious food, engaged in perfect work, knew absolute leisure, and delighted in communicating with God. In a word, they were *free*. Life could not have been any better.

Apparently, that was not enough for them. They wanted more. When they fell into sin, the devil spiritually imprisoned them and all humans, as referenced in the above scripture.

"Don't touch that hot stove, Johnny!" mommy and daddy lovingly warned the toddler. He smelled his favorite meal, macaroni and cheese.

He could not help himself. He just had to see his beloved macaroni boiling in the pot. He toddled into the kitchen and while mommy wasn't looking, reached up and pulled the pot with boiling water down onto himself. He was curious, chose not to obey, and was scalded.

The human race was more than scalded when Adam and Eve chose to fulfill their own desires, rather than obey their caring God. When they fulfilled their own lusts, their godly nature became a sinful nature and that nature was passed on to all humans. That sinful nature prompts us not to do what God wants us to do. It prevents us from living in the freedom God intended for us. In this way evil entered our world and brought death. Therefore, we all die.

Genesis 3:1-14 gives us the story. In verse 1, the devil showed up in the form of a slithering, talking snake. Look how smoothly the devil deceived Eve when he twisted God's loving and generous command.

God said, " . . . You may freely eat the fruit of every tree in the garden except . . . [one]" (Genesis 2:16) The cunning devil changed God's wording with his deceptive question, "Did God really say you must not eat the fruit from any of the trees . . .?" (Genesis 3:1)

Note that God used the word, "freely" with Adam, whereas the devil said, "not any" to Eve. God gave freedom, the devil brought a lie. God told Adam he could freely eat from every tree, except one. The devil purposefully misquoted God and implied that Adam and Eve were not allowed to eat from any tree.

Eve answered the devil, "Of course we may eat fruit from the trees in the garden . . . It's only the fruit from the tree in the middle of the garden that we are not allowed to eat. God said, 'You must not eat it or . . . you will die.'" (Genesis 3:2-3)

The devil immediately snapped back with his blunt lie in verse 4, "You won't die!" Then he went on to rationalize his answer to convince Eve that he was right. As he talked, Eve lingered and listened. She was lured by his lie that she would "be like God, knowing both good and evil." (Verse 5)

Knowing both good and evil implied that she would be freer than she already was at the time, because she knew only the good that God gave her. Knowing good *and evil* led her to believe she would have more freedom. She began to believe she could live a better life beyond the intimate relationship she already had with her all-supplying and loving God.

Lucifer charmed her like a Don Juan. He lured her until she was convinced that he was trustworthy. With intrigue flooding her innocent mind, she went to the forbidden tree and " . . . saw that the tree was beautiful and its fruit looked delicious and she wanted the wisdom it would give her." (Verse 6) She was hooked as she drank in its beauty. She knew a beautiful tree when she saw one. As she reached out, she picked its fruit, held it in her hands, looked at it, admired it, caressed it, and lusted for how it would taste and feel in her mouth. She bit into it. Ahhhh. It tasted *so good*. After she ate, she gave some to her husband. He undoubtedly had God's command ringing in his ears, "Don't eat the fruit from this one tree, if you do, you will die." (Genesis 2:17) Nevertheless, as he ate, he enjoyed the sensuous moment of culinary delight along with Eve.

Verse 7 gives the result. "At that moment their eyes were opened, and they suddenly felt shame . . ." Something was wrong, drastically wrong, and they intuitively knew it.

Thud.

This is the *Fall*—Adam and Eve fell into sin.

Immediately after the Fall, God came on the scene and asked Adam and Eve some questions. The conversation (Genesis 3:11-14) follows:

God asked, "Have you eaten from the tree whose fruit I commanded you not to eat?"

Adam replied, "It was the woman you gave me who gave me the fruit, and I ate it."

God turned to Eve and asked her, "What have you done?"

Eve replied, "The serpent deceived me . . . that's why I ate it."

Then God turned to the snake and cursed it. Note, God did not curse Adam and Eve.

When Adam and Eve fell, sin entered their lives and became their new nature. In that sinful nature, they blamed someone else and did not take responsibility for what each had done.

The Greek word for sin is *hamartia*, which literally means "to miss the mark." It is an archer's term for an arrow missing its target. What was the target that Adam and Eve missed when they sinned? It was the image of God.

For this discussion, *image* can be understood as ". . . the original purpose or blueprint from which they were created. This goes beyond wrong choices and lifestyles; it speaks to where . . . behavior originates. God revealed to Adam our human identity, the shape and form he intended for us, creating us in his own image and likeness (Genesis 1:26). Image means that Adam represented God-who-is-love to the rest of creation . . ."[8] As long as Adam and Eve mirrored God as love, they lived in the image of God.

However, when they went rogue and willfully disobeyed God, they chose to become independent of Him. With their greedy, selfish act, they missed the mark of portraying God as love. They fractured their perfect, loving relationship with God. After that, they no longer represented God as love because they were no longer living in a perfect loving relationship with Him. Satan deceived Adam and Eve into thinking they could break free from God and do their own thing.

They did not gain freedom with this act; they lost it. They traded their liberty in God for bondage to sin. The "fall" into sin has many repercussions. However, I want to focus on just one: the loss of freedom.

Adam and Eve traded their free and innocent nature for an imprisoned, guilty one. They scarred the human race all the way down to you and me.

Why did this happen?

It happened because the devil wanted to ruin God's perfect creation. When he showed up, slithered down the tree, and deceived Eve, he accomplished his goal. This is the worst story in the Bible. It screams the problem of evil, and who's behind everything that's wrong in our lives and the world. Evil is the most sinister problem we deal with and this story reveals who brought it to our world—the devil.

He has other names, such as the serpent, satan, lucifer, the accuser, and the dragon. He was an angel who rebelled against God in heaven. Many angels followed his lead. Consequently, God kicked him and his followers (commonly called demons), out of heaven and threw them down to the earth. "Then there was war in heaven. [The angel] Michael and his angels fought against the dragon and his angels. And the dragon lost the battle, and he and his angels were forced out of heaven. This great dragon—the ancient serpent, called the devil or satan, the one deceiving the whole world—was thrown down to the earth with all his angels." (Revelation 12:7-9)

The devil's demons follow his commands. Along with him, they are the spiritual forces that attack and influence humans. The devil and his army of demons unleash the dark, spiritual forces of sin, evil, and death on earth. This is why humanity has so many problems.

Beware! Sometimes, tornadoes come when the sky looks beautiful. Even partly cloudy and sunny skies look nice, but they can produce the right conditions for tornadoes, which can bring death and destruction.

On April 26, 1992, a tornado struck McConnell Air Force Base (AFB), in Wichita, Kansas. Carol and I lived in base housing. We heard the screeching siren warn us of the impending tornado. We immediately ran downstairs to the basement, where we listened to the newscaster on our portable radio. He described the tornado as "dancing over the flight line of the base and across Rock Road." It was headed right for us! Soon, we heard the roar of that monster. It was like a freight train bearing down and rumbling toward our neighborhood. I peeked out our basement window and saw the huge, gray, black, twisting monster on the ground heading in our direction. About a quarter mile away, it hit its first house, which exploded into a million pieces. Poof! Just like that, it was gone. The next house was hit and vanished, and another, and another . . . I was mesmerized.

Carol screamed at me to "get down here and cover up!" I did. We covered ourselves with blankets and luggage we had stored in the basement. We huddled together on the floor and held tightly to the suitcases as shields, hoping they would protect us from flying glass and debris. We prayed. The only part of the prayer I remember was, "Tornado, you have no power over us, we command you to leave!"

Instantly, an eerie silence followed . . . deafening silence. The monster had left. We slowly uncovered ourselves, afraid of what we might see. Everything was fine in the basement. We trudged upstairs. Everything was normal inside our house. The roof was still on and there were no broken windows. I ran to the door and with trembling fingers, opened it and saw disaster. Live power lines hung dangerously low. Some popped and danced as they touched the ground where sparks flew. Ruined houses stood dark and deathly silent. The neighborhood looked like a war zone. The children's playground was devoid of joyful screams or youthful shouts.

Likewise, disaster happened in the Garden of Eden. Life was perfect until the devil showed up and deceived Adam and Eve. The tornado of death and destruction blew into the garden. It was not like a loud, freight train—far worse. It came in the form of a silent, slithering, sneaky, swindling snake. His distortions fractured God's perfect creation. Adam and Eve fell for the lie, rebelled against God, quit displaying His image of love to the world, gave up their freedom, and imprisoned themselves and us in the devil's suffocating squeeze. Ever since, lucifer is the python squeezing life out of his helpless, captured prey—humans. We cannot escape by our own strength. We are helpless against the anaconda.

Immediately after Adam and Eve fell into the prison of sin, God initiated His plan to send His Son, Jesus, to free humanity from satan's grip. This freedom is at the center of the Bible's central message.

CHAPTER 5

Redemption: God Sets People Free

" . . . he will crush your head . . ." (Genesis 3:15 NIV)

BILL GAITHER RECORDED HOW Jesus brought freedom to the captured human race in the following song.

Let Freedom Ring
God built freedom into every fiber of creation
And he meant for us to all be free and whole
When my Lord bought freedom with the blood of His redemption
His cross stamped pardon on my very soul

I'll sing it out with every breath, I'll let the whole world hear it
This hallelujah anthem of the free
That iron bars and heavy chains can never hold us captive
The Son has made us free and free indeed[9]

Genesis 3:15 through Revelation 22:21 is the third component of the central message of the Bible. The first two components are Creation and the Fall. This portion of the message is the story of redemption:

God developing His plan *to send His Son, Jesus the Christ, into this world to free people from evil so He could restore them to Himself.* This is the remainder of the Bible.

Redemption means *restoration from captivity.* A thing does not need to be restored unless it is lost from its previous condition or owner. God was the previous owner, so to speak. He loved Adam and Eve with all His heart and He wanted to restore them to Himself.

God's love is a specific type of love called *agape* love. *Agape* love is that special love God has for people with eternity in His mind. It is salvation love. Through that love God shows humanity that He wants us to live with Him in eternity and not hell. (We will discuss other types of love in Chapter 15.)

The Lord did not intend for Adam and Eve to fall into the devil's prison of sin. After they sinned, God intended to restore them into the relationship they once had with Him. To accomplish this, God planned to release them from evil. That release would make it possible for them to return to Him and He would restore them to freedom.

Jesus fulfilled that plan when He came "to bring [people] safely home to God." (1 Peter 3:18) That redemptive theme becomes the central message that spans the rest of the Bible. It is all about God sending Jesus to our world to bring eternal salvation and freedom to all who believe in Him. Those who believed He would restore to Himself.

We study redemption in context with Creation and the Fall because those two events give us the information we need to correctly understand what it means to be restored from captivity.

This background lays the foundation for why we need a rescuer and shows us how unable we are to release ourselves from our imprisonment. We must have a liberator to set us free.

But, free from what? A better question might be: Free from whom? When Adam and Eve sinned, they traded in their God-given freedom for slavery to the devil. When that happened, God immediately initiated His plan, to free humanity from the devil's grip.

God revealed that plan within the context of three words: Creation, Fall and Redemption. The entire Bible can be summarized in these three words. These three components are our benchmarks for correctly understanding the entire Bible. This standard of reference will become self-evident as we follow the central message throughout scripture.

If we read the Bible within this context we will understand it much easier and quicker. We will grasp the intended, original meaning of stories and teachings throughout God's Word. This enables us to apply those teachings to ourselves with integrity. We will see numerous examples of this throughout our study.

Within this context we will trace God's plan to set humans free by studying key scripture references. I will put these references in **bold** type. They are listed in the appendix in the same order in which they appear in the Bible and this book, for quick and easy cross-reference. They are listed chronologically in the context of Creation, Fall and Redemption. The appendix will serve as the "spine" of the Bible.

We all have a spine, made up of individual vertebrae through which our spinal cord passes. Our spine is a part of our body that cannot be replaced. We can receive a new heart, other organs, graft in skin and arteries, but not our spine.

Our spinal cord is totally encased in bone. Similarly, the Bible's central message is totally encased in very specific scripture verses. The bold scripture references are verses that simulate vertebrae, through which the Bible's redemptive message passes from beginning to end. The spine of the Bible begins here.

Genesis 1:1-2:25 – *Creation:* God created a perfect universe.

Genesis 2:16-17 – God warned Adam and Eve not to eat from one tree in the Garden.

Genesis 3:1-14 – *Fall*: Adam and Eve did eat and gave up their God-given freedom.

Genesis 3:15 – Revelation 22:21 – *Redemption:* The remainder of the Bible is God's plan to restore people from captivity and bring them into His freedom.

Believe it or not, references to Jesus did not start with the New Testament! In fact, He was referred to as early as Genesis 3:15. The first thing God said about Jesus (without mentioning His name) was not salvation, but destruction. God promised that Jesus would come to this world to destroy the devil. It was after this message that God went on to develop His redemptive plan.

Redemption began in the Garden of Eden. God showed us His heart when He talked to the devil after the snake led Adam and Eve into sin. God said to His enemy, "And I will put enmity between you and the woman, and between your offspring and hers; he will crush your head, and you will strike his heel." (Genesis 3:15 NIV)

To "put enmity" means to cause hostility or war. This is how God started His redemptive plan. He loved Adam and Eve so much that He immediately declared war on the devil to eradicate him and set humanity free from his evil power. God would accomplish this redemptive plan by winning a celestial war against His enemy.

God had two goals in mind with His declaration in verse 15: He would destroy the devil, and bring redemption to humanity. He would accomplish both through Jesus. In this manner, God boldly predicted redemption for the first time in the Bible.

Imagine an angry God, fire in His eyes, red-faced, jaw set, neck veins bulging as He reprimanded the devil face-to-face in front of Adam and Eve. It was as if God said, "Since you mortally wounded my beloved Adam and Eve, you and I are at war and I will destroy you." (Genesis 3:15) God drew up the battle lines right then and there.

We can describe the hostility as war between God and the devil, between good and evil, angels and demons, and between humans and evil forces. It is the lifelong struggle that some have called "the problem of evil" or "the problem of sin." This conflict is captured in the question, "Why do bad things happen to good people?" One could also ask, "Why do good things happen to bad people?"

We are born into that struggle and experience it when we are tempted to do something wrong. For clarity, let's now refer to the hostility as "spiritual warfare," because it has come upon humans by spiritual forces and embroils all of us, whether we realize it or not. Sadly, people around the globe, including most Christians, are not aware that they are in this war.

After God drew the battle lines in Genesis 3:15a, in verse 15b, He told the devil, " . . . he will crush your head, and you will strike his heel." Notice that God starts this phrase with "he." This offspring is singular and refers to a specific person. I believe that person is Jesus and the Bible's central message will prove this.

God placed a curse on His enemy when He said, "Because you have done this (deceived Adam and Eve), you are cursed more than all animals, domestic and wild. You will crawl on your belly and grovel in the dust as long as you live." (Genesis 3:14)

Can you imagine how Adam and Eve must have felt when they heard God tell the devil, right in front of them, that someone would come to crush his head? The news that someone would come to wipe out their enemy, who had just mortally wounded them, had to lift their spirits. God did not curse them. When He said, " . . . he will crush your head . . ." He cursed their attacker and gave them hope for redemption.

The plan for redemption that began in the garden will come to completion in the book of Revelation. Redemption was God's intent from the very beginning. That intent will become reality in the end when

Jesus destroys the devil. "The devil, who had deceived them, was thrown into the fiery lake of burning sulfur . . ." (Revelation 20:10)

It is good to know that God will ultimately destroy the devil. Knowing satan's end, at the hands of Jesus, gives us courage and confidence because Jesus is stronger than our enemy. He is more than able to free us from the devil's imprisoning grip. As we go to Him, we receive that freedom.

That said, the devil will not give up without a fight. The next phrase, "and you will strike his heel," means the snake could only strike the man's heel. A man walks upright and can crush a snake's head as it crawls in the dust. However, the snake on the ground can only strike what he can reach, in this case, the man's heel. This difference between man and snake " . . . is itself the result of the curse pronounced upon the serpent, and its crawling in the dust is a sign that it will be defeated in its conflict with man. However pernicious [venomous] may be the bite of a serpent in the heel when the poison circulates throughout the body, it is not immediately fatal and utterly incurable, like the crushing of a serpent's head."[10]

The snake (devil) would strike Jesus' heel. What does this mean? This refers to Jesus' suffering at the end of His earthly life, when religious leaders and politicians along with soldiers ridiculed, beat, and whipped Him. Then Roman soldiers crucified and killed Him. Through those events, the devil figuratively bit Jesus' heel and wounded Him.

Thank God, the story did not end there! The devil only wounded Jesus. He did not defeat Jesus because He rose from the dead, thereby ripping away the devil's power over death. Jesus proved Himself to be stronger than the devil and will eventually destroy him.

In this chapter, we learned that God began His plan to set us free from the devil's grip with a promise to send a person to this world who would destroy the devil. How and when would He send that person into our world? In the next chapter, we will learn the beginning of the process that launched Jesus into our world.*

*Note: To impress on us the reality of God working His redemptive plan throughout the history of this world, from now on, I include an approximate date under each chapter title to give a time line to the steps in that plan. The Bible provides some information on dates for the events but not enough to give us a detailed picture. Therefore, the dates are approximate. My intention is to give the reader a feel for God's work throughout history, not to be dogmatic on specific dates. As best as we can, we will follow God through the Bible in an orderly and historical fashion from Genesis through Revelation as He develops His redemptive plan.

CHAPTER 6

Souled out to God (Approximately 2000 BC)

"And Abram believed the Lord, and the Lord counted him as righteous because of his faith." (Genesis 15:6)

GOD WOVE THE MESSAGE of redemption throughout the Bible. Genesis 3:15 is the start of that plan. We saw in the last chapter that God promised the devil He would destroy him through Eve's offspring: Jesus. How would He accomplish this?

God would choose individuals throughout history to be the bloodline through whom Jesus would enter our world to accomplish redemption. God chose Abram and his wife, Sarai, to begin that process. They would become the grandparents of Jacob who birthed the nation of Israel. Israel became the nation from which Jesus would be born.

"The Lord had said to Abram, 'Leave your native country, your relatives, and your father's family, and go to the land that I will show you. I will make you into a great nation. I will bless you and make you famous, and you will be a blessing to others. I will bless those who bless you and curse those who treat you with contempt. All the families on earth will be blessed through you.'" **(Genesis 12:1-3)**

At that time Abram was seventy-five years old and married to Sarai who was sixty-five. They were beyond childbearing years and Sarai had not been able to conceive a child.

Only God could build a nation from a childless couple . . . and that is the point! God created this scenario to show His dynamic power. He would demonstrate that He is God because only He could successfully pull off this unfathomable plan. To top it off, He would perform the unimaginable through the obedience of people who trusted Him. Notice that Abram did not question God. He simply moved to Canaan as he was told.

Galatians 3:8 (around 49 AD) is the fulfillment of this prophecy, "What's more, the Scriptures looked forward to this time when . . . God proclaimed this good news to Abraham long ago when he said, 'All nations will be blessed through you.'" God developed His plan even further when He announced that all the families of the earth would be blessed through Abraham. That includes the family of the person reading this book.

God made the blessing of all nations possible in **Genesis 15:1-6**. He showed that He would work His plan of salvation through the Jewish people, who were descendants of Abram.

Abram asked God, " . . . what good are all your blessings when I don't even have a son?" (Verse 2) God replied, " . . . you will have a son of your own who will be your heir." (Verse 4) Then, the Lord took Abram outside and said to him, "Look up into the sky and count the stars if you can. That is how many descendants you will have!" (Verse 5) With this, God predicted Abram and Sarai, childless at the time, would become the parents of so many descendants that Abram would not be able to count them all.

Abram responded by believing God. (Verse 6) In the same verse, God "counted him as righteous because of his faith." In this interaction, Abram demonstrated that he was sold out to God and he was credited for his faith. We could say Abram was not only *sold out* to God, but *souled out* to Him. Believing God would give him and his wife countless ancestors had to take a soul that was entirely "souled out" to God.

Next, God appeared to Abram in **Genesis 17:1-7.** In verses 1 and 2, He said, " . . . I am El-Shaddai—God Almighty. Serve me faithfully and live a blameless life. I will make a covenant with you by which I will guarantee to give you countless descendants . . . I will make you the father of a multitude of nations!" God explained to Abram that he would not be the father of only one nation—Israel, but a *multitude* of nations. As an assurance, the Lord made a covenant with him.

The word covenant means "to cut." In Old Testament times, covenants were "made" or "cut." When two parties entered a covenant, both would often cut themselves to produce blood. This was a graphic expression of the commitment that one would die before he broke the covenant.

With that in mind, a covenant is a binding arrangement and relationship between two parties. It is more than a simple agreement to do a task for someone. Both parties are bound by their oath and each has a costly responsibility to make that covenant work. To break a covenant would require a heavy cost, such as blood or even one's life.

God's responsibility was to give countless descendants to Abram in every generation throughout history. Abram's responsibility was to believe God.

God said, "What's more, I am changing your name. It will no longer be Abram. Instead, you will be called Abraham, for you will be the father of many nations. I will make you extremely fruitful." (verses 5 and 6) Abraham literally means "father of many." He would become the father of many nations. To achieve this, God healed Sarai so she could become pregnant.

Genesis chapters 12, 15, and 17 show the increase in the number of Abraham's descendants. In these chapters, we see his descendants grow from a single son, to the nation of Israel, to countless descendants, to a multitude of nations. God indeed had something big in mind. The Bible's central message of freedom for humanity was well on its way.

The story continues. God said, "I will confirm my covenant with you and your descendants after you, from generation to generation. This is the everlasting covenant: I will always be your God and the God of your descendants after you." (Genesis 17:7) Many call this "the covenant of grace" because God states His intent to be gracious to Abraham's descendants throughout history. It is as if God said, "You can take my promise to the bank; you can count on it." He went so far that He said His covenant would be "everlasting," or without end. Here we see a hint of eternity.

Until this point, we have only talked about physical children born to physical parents. Abraham and Sarah would have a son named Isaac. Isaac fathered Jacob, who became the direct patriarch of the nation of Israel. It is amazing how Abram and Sarai became Abraham and Sarah and gave birth to an entire nation. But there is more; the plot thickens.

Abraham and Sarah would not only have physical, Jewish children who had faith in God. Through Jesus, they would have non-Jewish, spiritual children; those people from nations and races around the globe who believed in Jesus for their salvation and freedom. "So, Abraham is the spiritual father of those who have faith . . . They are counted as righteous because of their faith." **(Romans 4:11)**

The connection between Abraham's physical and spiritual children is as follows: Abraham fathered the nation of Israel. These people were his physical descendants. Jesus was born from that nation, and therefore He was also a physical descendant of Abraham. (Matthew 1:1, 2 and Luke 3:23, 34) However, Jesus became the Redeemer for all nations in the world, which is a lot more than only Israel.

Those nations were known as "Gentiles" by the Jewish people. Throughout history many people come to God from those Gentile nations. They come to God by believing in Jesus as their Savior and Lord. Their faith in God through Jesus makes them spiritual descendants of Abraham because, like Abraham, they have faith in God.

As Abraham believed the Lord, God counted his faith as righteousness. The same is true for us. As we believe the Lord, God counts our faith as righteousness. In this sense Abraham is our spiritual father, because we believe God as he did.

The promise of salvation and freedom is focused in Jesus Christ. The apostle Paul taught "God gave the promises to Abraham and his child. Notice the scripture doesn't say, 'to his children,' as if it meant many descendants. Rather, it says, 'to his child'—and that, of course, means Christ." **(Galatians 3:16)** The word *child* is singular, not plural; therefore, God gave His promises to Abraham and his child, Jesus, the Christ. (In this text, the word *child* is translated "seed or offspring" in some Bible translations.)

The word "Christ" means *Messiah*, or "Anointed One." Jesus became the Anointed One who brought salvation and freedom to the people of the world. This is what God referred to when He said, "all the families on earth will be blessed through you." (Genesis 12:3) As such, God's blessing of salvation and freedom flows from Him through Jesus into all the nations of the world. God confirmed this when He said, "You will be the father of many nations." (Genesis 17:5) Jesus would be the individual through whom all the families on earth would be blessed if they believed in Him.

Believers in Jesus are spread throughout the world in many nations. They are "all the families" who "will be blessed" through Abraham, as prophesied in Genesis 12:3 and 17:4, 5.

God brought all this together in His prophecy, namely: "I will confirm my covenant with you and your offspring (singular) after you from generation to generation. This is the everlasting covenant: I

45

will always be your God and the God of your descendants after you."
(Genesis 17:7)

People who trust Jesus for eternal freedom have the God of Abraham as their God because He is the One who sent Jesus.

When we believe God through faith as Abraham did, we become part of God's family. We enter God's plan of salvation ourselves. At this point, it is no longer only a theory or story in the Bible; it is personal because it is the story of our eternal life.

God brought the Old Testament (OT) and New Testament (NT) together in His central message. Note the truth in the Old Testament column below is fulfilled in the New Testament column.

Old Testament	New Testament
Genesis 12:3 " . . . All the families on earth will be blessed through you."	Galatians 3:8 "God proclaimed this good news to Abraham long ago when he said, 'All nations will be blessed through you.'"
Genesis 15:6 "And Abram believed the Lord, and the Lord counted him as righteous because of his faith."	Galatians 3:5,6 "It is because you believe the message you heard about Christ. In the same way, 'Abraham believed God, and God counted him as righteous because of his faith.' The real children of Abraham, then, are those who put their faith in God."

Genesis 17:7 "I will confirm my covenant with you and your seed . . . "	Galatians 3:16 "God gave the promises to Abraham and . . . 'to his child' [seed] and that, of course, means Christ.'"

God birthed, (brought into existence) the nation of Israel from Abraham's and Sarah's loins. They brought their son, Isaac, into the world. Isaac fathered Jacob, the patriarch who had twelve sons. From those sons and their wives came twelve tribes that made up the nation of Israel. Jesus came from that nation. From which tribe within that nation would He come?

CHAPTER 7

Most Favored Nation Status (1800 BC?)

"The scepter will not depart from Judah, nor . . . from his descendants . . ." (Genesis 49:10)

IN 1995, THE AIR force assigned me to Headquarters U.S. European Command, Stuttgart, Germany. One of our responsibilities was to determine which nations we would place on a "Most Favored Nation Status" list. Nations clamored to be on that list for its many benefits, such as economic, political, diplomatic, cultural, and social assistance.

Comparatively, but on a much greater scale, God decided which tribe in Israel He would favor to bring the Messiah into this world. "He chose . . . the tribe of Judah." (Psalm 78:68)

In this chapter, we will learn about the next step in God's freedom plan. We will discover how God determined the "most favored nation status" for the tribe of Judah and why that tribe would be the one from whom the Savior would come. Once God chose Judah, He kept that tribe at the center of His plan through the remainder of the Bible. This is important. It showed that God could be trusted. He consistently carried out His promises to Judah through the end of the plan. In fact, God also proved He is trustworthy to us, because He logically and steadily carried out every detail to make good on His promise to send the liberator as He said He would in Genesis 3:15.

God's plan of redemption began when God said someone would come to destroy the devil. (Genesis 3:15) God promised a son to Abraham in Genesis 15:4. The one who would destroy the devil would come from Abraham's descendants.

Genesis 49:10 reveals the next piece of God's plan: "The scepter will not depart from Judah, nor the ruler's staff from his descendants, until the coming of the one to whom it belongs, the one whom all nations will honor." The speaker in this scripture was the patriarch Jacob, who was Abraham's grandson. As Jacob was about to die, he called his sons together so he could speak his parting blessing on each of them.

When he came to his fourth son, Judah, Jacob told his children that the Messiah would come from Judah's tribe. (Genesis 49:10) Why the fourth son and not the first, second, or third? According to the culture of the day, the firstborn should have been the one to produce the Messiah. Reuben, the firstborn, was passed over because he had committed incest. Simeon and Levi, sons two and three, had also committed crimes. Therefore, Jacob came to Judah and blessed him with the promise that Jesus would come from his tribe. This promise was repeated throughout the rest of the Bible. It became central to Jewish teaching that the Messiah would come from the tribe of Judah.

Jacob said, "Judah, my son, is a young lion that has finished eating its prey. Like a lion he crouches and lies down; like a lioness—who dares to rouse him?" (Genesis 49:9) Judah showed strength and courage, which caused his dad to think of him as a lion. For example, he saved his brother Joseph's life by talking his brothers into selling him instead of killing him. (Genesis 37:26-28) At another time, Judah offered himself as a hostage for the safety of his youngest brother, Benjamin. (Genesis

43:9) By these actions, and probably many others, he showed moral strength. He stood strong as a lion in the face of evil, to conquer wrong and do right. He was a savior, of sorts, to his brothers; strong enough to save their lives and courageous enough to stand in the face of difficulty. He was a leader.

Jacob rewarded Judah when he said, " . . . the scepter . . . the ruler's staff . . . will not depart from Judah or his descendants . . . " (Verse 10) Leadership would never leave the tribe of Judah. The scepter and ruler's staff are the same, and symbolize rulership. The scepter was a rod (or wand) a ruler carried as a symbol of authority. The king would have stood it between his feet or next to him as he sat on his throne. When a person asked permission to speak to the king, the ruler would decide if he wanted to hear what that person had to say or if he would dismiss him. If he decided to hear the subject, he would pick up the scepter, point it toward the person, and then lower it as a sign that the requester was welcome in his presence and was allowed to speak. Judah would have that power.

Jacob went on to say in the same verse, " . . . until the coming of the one to whom it belongs, the one whom all nations will honor." The scepter, which represented leadership, belonged to an unnamed ruler and it would not depart from Judah until its owner came to claim it.

God fulfilled this prophecy approximately two thousand years later; that owner proved to be Jesus, the Messiah. At the appointed time, Jesus came to earth. He was born of the tribe of Judah, in the town of Bethlehem. Upon His arrival, He symbolically took the ruler's staff and began His rule. All nations will eventually honor Him.

How was this possible? Throughout history in the Old Testament, God reminded the Bible reader that the Messiah would come from the tribe of Judah. Later, God refined this prophecy when He added the throne of King David to it. David was the greatest king of the tribe of Judah. To understand the importance of the prophecy that Jesus would come from the tribe of Judah, we will see below how God worked His plan over a two-thousand-year period. The timelines are as follows:

- Genesis 49:10: The prediction that the Messiah would come from the tribe of Judah.
- 2 Samuel 2:4: "Then the men of Judah came to David and anointed him king over the people of Judah."
- 2 Samuel 7:16: God said to King David: "Your house and your kingdom will continue before me for all time, and your throne will be secure forever."
- 1 Kings 2:4: King David was dying and told his son, Solomon, what God told him years earlier: "If your descendants live as they should and follow me faithfully with all their heart and soul, one of them will always sit on the throne of Israel."
- 1 Kings 12:19, 20: "And to this day the northern tribes of Israel have refused to be ruled by a descendant of David . . . only the tribe of Judah remained loyal to the family of David."
- Micah 5:2: "But you, O Bethlehem . . . are only a small village among all the people of Judah. Yet a ruler of Israel will come from you . . ."
- Matthew 2:1: "Jesus was born in Bethlehem in Judea . . ."

There you have it! Almost two thousand years after the plan was introduced, Jesus was born from the tribe of Judah through the throne of King David. With Jesus' birth, God completed Judah's part in the plan of salvation, " . . . Look, the Lion of the tribe of Judah . . . has won the victory." (Revelation 5:5)

Judah was at the center of God's plan from Genesis to Revelation. The scepter of authority belongs to Jesus and He still wields it. With His authority, He builds the Kingdom of God, causes people to repent of their wrongdoing, forgives sins, heals the sick, casts out demons, raises the dead, and a host of other signs, wonders, and miracles.

God made it clear how His plan would finish during the last days in Revelation. (Revelation 22:16) Jesus is the Lion of the Tribe of Judah, who continues to gain victory over His enemies and brings freedom to His people around the world. That is the history of the entire world in a snapshot! It is the greatest story ever told!

CHAPTER 8

I AM the Exodus (1446 BC)

" . . . I have certainly seen the oppression of my people . . . So, I have come down to rescue them . . . Now go, for I am sending you to . . . lead my people . . . out." (Exodus 3:7, 8, 10)

YES, IT IS QUITE a story. In the last chapter, we saw Jesus fulfill Judah's role in God's plan. However, God had other elements in His plan that had to occur before Jesus came on the scene.

The time from Abraham to the Exodus was roughly 720 years (2166 BC to 1446 BC). This was the incubation period that God used to birth Israel into His chosen nation. Through Israel, He showed His power to the people of Egypt. This was a precursor to God demonstrating His greatest power to the entire world through His Son, Jesus.

During those years in Egypt, God used a group of slaves in Egypt to form the nation of Israel. For Israel to fulfill her destiny to birth the Messiah, God had to first free her from bondage in Egypt. He chose a man to lead His people out of slavery and guide them to the land He promised to give them. God chose an adopted baby to become the leader of the nation of Israel—a man called Moses.

We have the story in **Exodus 3:1-14.** God spoke to Moses from a burning bush. This story is special to me because I once lived in the parched Saudi Arabian Desert, which is next to the arid Sinai Peninsula where Moses met God at the burning bush. The U.S. Air Force assigned me to Riyadh, the capital city of Saudi Arabia. During that time, I regularly traveled to remote areas across the barren desert to visit my troops. There was mostly sand, rocks, and dirt, but not much vegetation. With few plants in sight, I wondered how a burning bush could become a reality in such a barren place. Bushes that did grow in the extreme heat and arid climate were very small, spindly, and scraggly. If they were to catch fire, they would not last more than a couple of minutes in the intense, dry, desert heat. When I saw one of these little bushes, I wondered, *how could it blaze with fire like the bush Moses saw?*

In 1446 BC, Moses was an unsuspecting shepherd in a Middle Eastern desert, known today as the Sinai Peninsula, west of the Arabian Desert. There was not much excitement in the vast, lonely, hot, dry desert. There was not much to look forward to when your days were spent with a bunch of boring sheep.

Then, all heaven broke loose! Only God could make a scraggly bush burst into flames at precisely the right place and time so Moses would see the blaze as he ambled by with his sheep. Exodus 3:2 described it as "a blazing fire." Surely Moses saw and heard the brambles and thorns pop and crackle as they exploded into the air.

I would be totally mesmerized if I saw a burning bush in the Saudi Desert. Imagine, one little bush, virtually no other plant life or people around, growing in dry ground, and poof—it burst into flames on its own? No wonder Moses was intrigued when he saw it. Indeed, God caught his attention. If that wasn't enough, the surprised Moses saw that the fire *did not consume* the bush!

Amazed, Moses asked himself, "Why isn't that bush burning up?" (Exodus 3:3)

He was hooked. He was so fascinated that curiosity got the best of him and intrigue drove him to take a closer look. Moses probably said to himself, "I've gotta see this!"

As he approached, God scared him out of his desert sandals when He spoke from within the burning bush. "Moses! Moses! . . . Do not come any closer . . . Take off your sandals, for you are standing on holy ground. I am the God of your father—the God of Abraham, the God of Isaac, and the God of Jacob." (Exodus 3:5,6)

God caught Moses' attention not only with a blazing bush that didn't burn up, but also with His voice, which came from the middle of the bush. When Moses heard Him, he covered his face because he was afraid to look. (Verse 6)

Then God launched the next missile in His fight for our freedom. He told Moses that He planned to rescue His people from Egypt and bring them to the promised land. Then He hit Moses right between the eyes when He told him that he would be the guy to make it happen.

Moses protested. Twice. He stammered, "If I go to the people of Israel and tell them, 'The God of your ancestors has sent me to you,' they will ask me, 'What is his name?' Then what should I tell them?'" (Verses 11-13)

God replied, "'I AM WHO I AM.' Say this to the people of Israel. I AM has sent me to you.'" (Verse 14)

How subtle, yet thunderously important, was this exchange between God and Moses. The name "I AM" is loaded with meaning. That is why my experience in the Saudi Desert made the story of Moses at the burning bush come alive, incredibly alive. I felt God's supernatural presence when the Saudi bushes reminded me of Moses at the burning bush. I hope the blazing bush story burns in your heart as it has in mine.

In **John 8:31-59,** Jesus talked to a crowd of Jews, including Pharisees and teachers of religious law (Verses 2-3) about their claim that Abraham was their father. Jesus said the Son could set them free from sin, which was a reference to Himself. (Verses 34-36) He told them He came from God. (Verse 42) Toward the end of the conversation, Jesus said to them, "I tell you the truth, before Abraham was even born, I AM!" (Verse 58)

The Jewish people knew God called Himself I AM at the burning bush. It was a well-known scripture. Through oral tradition, they handed down stories like this one, from generation to generation. When Jesus told them, "before Abraham was even born, I AM!" He was telling them He was God. Connecting the two references to the name I AM in Exodus 3:14 and John 8:58, we see that Jesus is God made visible to mankind. He spoke to Moses from the burning bush and He spoke to the Jews approximately 1,476 years later.

This truth that Jesus is *the* I AM, is critical for us to know. If Jesus is God, then He is the One all people need to come to in faith. There is no one else. Therefore, there is no other way to salvation and freedom from evil. Jesus said, "I am the way, the truth, and the life. No one can come to the Father except through me." (John 14:6) Belief in Jesus is a matter of eternal life and death. John 8:58 shows that Jesus *is* the main character in the Bible's central message of salvation and freedom. *I AM the Exodus* is an apt title for Jesus. He is the One who leads people in their exodus out of slavery into His promised land.

He surprised Moses at the crackling, burning bush. He worked through him to lead His people out of Egypt to freedom.

CHAPTER 9

The King Is Coming (930 BC?)

God said to David, "Your house and your kingdom will continue before me for all time, and your throne will be secure forever." (2 Samuel 7:16)

GOD'S APPEARANCE TO MOSES at the burning bush ushered in momentous events in biblical history, including the Exodus, the Ten Commandments, and forty years of Israel wandering through the desert. During their trip to the promised land, God spoke to the nation of Israel: "I am the Lord your God, who brought you out of the land of Egypt so you would no longer be their slaves. I broke the yoke of slavery from your neck so you can walk with your heads held high." (Leviticus 26:13) They were free.

They would have remained free if they obeyed God on their journey, but they disobeyed and paid the price by wandering forty years in the wilderness. When God sets us free from evil, we are still called to obedience. As we obey we can continue to walk with our heads held high.

Years later, as the Israelites prepared to enter the promised land, Moses died. God appointed Joshua to lead the Israelites. Joshua masterfully helped defeat their enemies and the Israelite tribes settled into their respective locations.

Joshua's name in Hebrew was Jeshua, which is the same name as Jesus in Greek. Jeshua and Jesus convey "the idea that God delivers or saves His people."[11] This was the very purpose for which God sent Jesus to the earth. "And she [Mary] will have a son, and you are to name him Jesus for he will save his people from their sins." (Matthew 1:21) Due to the magnitude of His saving work on earth, He is the central person in the Bible. In a sense, Joshua was a type, or example, of Christ, because his actions were like Jesus leading His people into freedom.

After Joshua died, God appointed judges and kings to rule Israel. These leaders were responsible to lead the people to love, follow, and obey God. As long as Israel did this, they lived in a healthy relationship with God. He, in turn, fulfilled the promises He made earlier to Abraham—that He would bless him with a son through whom he would have countless descendants, both Jews and non-Jews (Gentiles). As long as Israel believed and worshipped God, they obeyed Him. "Yet Israel did not listen to the judges but prostituted themselves by worshiping other gods. How quickly they turned away from the path of their ancestors, who had walked in obedience to the Lord's commands." (Judges 2:17)

While Israel lived in the promised land, we see the next stage in God's plan for our freedom. The Almighty chose this time in biblical history to announce His plan that the Messiah would come from the family of King David, which was part of the tribe of Judah. We saw an action shot of this in chapter 7, Most Favored Nation Status.

God ensured that David would be anointed as the successor to the throne in Judah while his predecessor, King Saul, still reigned from that throne. Therefore, God commanded Samuel, Israel's spiritual leader and judge, to anoint David as the next king of Israel. (1 Samuel 16:12-13)

Why the prophetic anointing? Because Saul had rejected God's command to clean up sin in the nation of Israel. God wanted a man on the throne who would love Him and obey His commands. He found David who was " . . . a man after his own heart." (1 Samuel 13:14)

2 Samuel 2: 1-7 tells the story of the men of Judah anointing David as their king. This fulfilled Jacob's prophecy (Genesis 49:10) that the Messiah would come from Judah. God said to David, "Your house and your kingdom will continue before me for all time, and your throne will be secure forever." **(2 Samuel 7:16)**

There you have it. David would not last forever, but God promised that his throne would. With this promise, God established David's throne for eternity. The rest of the Old Testament and the New Testament repeat this promise over and over again. How would that throne become eternal? When the Messiah, Jesus, comes and establishes the Kingdom of God that has no end.

David's throne would last forever through his son, Solomon. Therefore, from Solomon onward, we see the plan of David's royal line continuing through Judean kings until Jesus came on the scene as the Anointed One to inherit King David's throne. **(1 Kings 9:4-5)**

Jesus was born from the Davidic line. "You will conceive and give birth to a son, and you will name him Jesus. He will be very great and will be called the Son of the Most High. The Lord God will give him the throne of his ancestor David. And he will reign over Israel forever; his Kingdom will never end!" **(Luke 1:31-33)** Here we have the "forever package."

John, Jesus' closest friend wrote, "For the Scriptures clearly state that the Messiah will be born of the royal line of David, in Bethlehem, the village where King David was born." (John 7:42) This prophecy of the Davidic line culminates in the very last chapter of the last book of the Bible, "I am both the source of David and the heir to his throne." (Revelation 22:16)

God developed His plan from the wide to the narrow, from the many to the individual. He started that plan when He promised

Abraham would father the nation of Israel. That nation would birth the Messiah. He narrowed it down from the nation to the tribe of Judah, and further slimmed it down to the Davidic line. This culminated in the individual—the Messiah, Jesus the Christ.

Beginning with Jesus, we see the plan going in the opposite direction, from the narrow to the broad and from the individual to the masses. God planned to bring freedom from one person to the entire globe. From Jesus, the Messiah, to billions of people in all nations.

The plot thickens. In addition to birthing the Messiah into this world, Israel was also responsible to tell the world about their God. **(1 Kings 8:41-43, 60-61)** The setting of the story is King Solomon dedicating the newly built temple to God. In one part of his dedication prayer, he implied that Israel would tell foreigners about God and the wonderful things He did for them. He also spoke of how those strangers would respond.

> "In the future, foreigners who do not belong to your people Israel will hear of you . . . they will hear of your great name and your strong hand and your powerful arm. And when they pray toward this Temple, then hear from heaven where you live, and grant what they ask of you. In this way, all the people of the earth will come to know and fear you, just as your own people Israel do . . . Then people all over the earth will know that the Lord alone is God and there is no other . . . " (1 Kings 8:41-43, 60)

God planned this to result in such good news that nations would hear about Israel's God. They would hear His great name, see His strong hand and powerful arm, and learn how He had taken care of His people, Israel. How would the nations hear that message? The Israelites would tell them about God's mighty acts, such as the Exodus and the Ten Commandments. In response, those countries would pray toward the temple in Jerusalem and ask God to grant what they asked for in prayer.

In this way, the people of the earth would hear about God and come to Him by faith, just as Abraham had done. This is recorded as part of King Solomon's prayer at the dedication of the temple. (1 Kings 8:41-43)

This is evangelism in the Old Testament. Not only did God desire to save His chosen people Israel, but also the *other* children of Abraham, those Gentiles who would come to God by faith as Abraham had. (Genesis 15:6) In the Old Testament, this was the salvation the Jews were supposed to bring to the world. In the New Testament, the Jewish nation was to proclaim the Messiah, who would bring salvation to the world. He would become the Savior of all Jews and non-Jews who believed in Him.

In regard to Israel's purpose in God's plan to redeem His universe, their entire history can be summarized in the genealogy of Jesus. Yes, the genealogy. What may appear to be boring lists of names now have purpose—real, meaningful purpose. Matthew 1:1-16 gives the genealogy from Abraham to Jesus, while Luke 3:23-38 lists the genealogy from Jesus and goes back through Abraham to Adam, all the way to God.

The next pieces of fabric God stitched into His master plan for freedom are those perfect predictions that prophets spoke about Jesus. Prophets proved to be the gutsiest people in the Old Testament. They spoke the truth fearlessly about the Messiah. Many were formidable: fearless, bold, robust, powerful, in-your-face, Spirit-filled people of God. They took the message of freedom to a higher level as they went on the offensive and confronted evil.

CHAPTER 10

Predicting the Coming King (700 BC?)

"But I carry out the predictions of my prophets!" (Isaiah 44:26)

"SOMETIMES, THE LONGEST AND most lonely walk is the one where you leave the presence of people and head toward the presence of God."[12] This was often true for prophets in the Old Testament. They did and said what God wanted them to do and say. Many people rejected the prophets and their message because they often told their targeted audiences the opposite of what they wanted to hear. The people of Israel did not appreciate hearing that their religious acts, such as bringing gifts to God, celebrating religious holidays, acting spiritual while they were fasting, or performing expected religious rituals, were not always what God wanted from them.

The prophets were sent to speak the truth to turn the people back to God. Prophets were counter-culture, counter-social, and counter-religious. That is why so many were outcasts, hated, persecuted, and some were even killed. In addition to telling Israel about their misdeeds, these bold proclaimers also brought the message of the coming Christ. They relentlessly gave perfect predictions because they spoke exactly what God told them to say. Even though the sin-darkened world did not want to hear what they had to say and persecuted them, these bold, fearless men unflinchingly spoke the truth that someone was coming to eradicate evil and set people free from its clutches.

"Come now, let us reason together, says the Lord. 'Though your sins are like scarlet, they shall be as white as snow; though they are red as crimson, they shall be like wool.'" (Isaiah 1:18, NIV) Here we see God's heart. He *wanted* to reason with the rebellious Israelites and work things out. He *wanted* to save them from eternal, imprisoned death and give them freedom along with eternal life. With this in mind, let's look at two prophecies that spoke of God bringing freedom to earth.

1. God spoke to the Israelites through the prophet Jeremiah. "You will be in Babylon for seventy years. But then I will come and do for you all the good things I have promised, and I will bring you home again. For I know the plans I have for you . . . They are plans for good and not for disaster, to give you a future and a hope." **(Jeremiah 29:10-11)**

God told the Israelites that He had plans, but did not explain those plans to the Israelites any further than to bring them back home to where they lived before their exile. However, His plans were not simply to bring Israel home again. He had another huge surprise for His beloved people. He would include all of history into one main plan for how He would redeem the world. He would bring the one mediator between God and humanity into this world through His people, Israel. He told them He knew the plans He had for them and they were good plans (Jeremiah 29:11) Good news for Israel and good news for the world. Here's why.

Approximately 660 years later the apostle Paul wrote, "God has now revealed to us his mysterious plan regarding Christ, a plan to fulfill his own good pleasure. *And this is the plan:* (emphasis mine) At the right time he will bring everything together under the authority of Christ—everything in heaven and on earth." **(Ephesians 1:9-10)**

There you have the explanation of God's plan of salvation. "At the right time, He will bring everything together under the authority of Christ . . ." Think of it! God our Father will bring everything together under Jesus' authority—everything. Jesus already had power over the devil. That is why He could forgive people of their sins and bring them salvation and freedom. But God will also bring everything under the authority of Christ at the end of time, when Jesus will conquer and destroy all His enemies. (Revelation 19 and 20) We will discuss that in a later chapter.

For our purpose in this chapter, let's acknowledge that Jesus has ultimate authority over everything. All the plans God had in the Old Testament converged into that one plan in the New Testament, when Jesus came to this earth to set humans free from the devil's evil grip. That made Jesus the centerpiece in God's plan to redeem people of faith, which is why He is the main character in the Bible.

"For God loved the world so much that he gave his one and only Son, so that everyone who believes in him will not perish but have eternal life." (**John 3:16**) All eternity revolves around Jesus. Everyone who believes in Him will have eternal life.

Biblical prophecy often has more than one level of interpretation. There is not only the literal, but also the spiritual. Therefore, God's plans (in Jeremiah 29:11) pertain not only to bringing Israel back to their homeland, but also to leading spiritual Israel (those children of Abraham who had faith in God) to their homeland—eternity with God. The Almighty promised throughout the Old Testament to send the Messiah to this world, to Jews and non-Jews, who believe in that Messiah. From His position of total authority, Jesus grants eternity to all who believe in Him from around the world. I believe this is what God prophesied through Jeremiah when He said, "I know the plans I have for you."

In summary, the plural plans meant the Israelites would come home, not only to their homeland in Palestine, but also find their home in God. This same truth of finding a home in God holds true for non-Jewish believers around the globe.

2. In the second prophecy the Babylonian king, Nebuchadnezzar, had a bad dream that really bothered him. He called his wise men, magicians, enchanters, sorcerers, and astrologers, and demanded that they tell him what he had dreamed and the interpretation to that dream. **(Daniel 2:31-45)** None could, except Daniel. He told the king what he had dreamt.

"In your vision, Your Majesty, you saw standing before you a huge, shining statue of a man . . . The head of the statue was made of gold, its chest and arms were silver, its belly and thighs were bronze, its legs were iron and its feet were a combination of iron and baked clay. As you watched, a rock was cut from a mountain but not by human hands. It struck the feet of iron and clay, smashing them to bits. The whole statue was crushed into small pieces . . . Then the wind blew them away without a trace . . . But the rock that knocked the statue down became a great mountain that covered the whole earth." (Daniel 2:31-35)

Most, if not all, theologians agree on the following interpretation of the dream. The first kingdom, of gold, represented the Babylonian kingdom; the second, of silver, became the empire of the Medes and Persians; the third, of bronze, was the Greek Empire under Alexander the Great; then came the Roman Empire, of iron. The feet of iron and clay are open to speculation, but many see them as the time from the close of the Roman Empire to the second coming of Christ.

The point of the prophecy is this: "During the reigns of those kings, the God of heaven will set up a kingdom that will never be destroyed or conquered. It will crush all these kingdoms into nothingness, and it will stand forever." (Daniel 2:44)

The rock, which was cut out of the mountain without human hands and rolled down and destroyed all the other kingdoms, represented the Kingdom of God. Jesus is the King who came to set up that Kingdom. His kingdom will supersede all others and last forever. " . . . The world has now become the Kingdom of our Lord and of his Christ, and he will reign forever and ever." **(Revelation 11:15)**

To make that happen, Jesus had to be born first. Micah predicted the Messiah would be born in Bethlehem of Judea. **(Micah 5: 2)** This was fulfilled in **Matthew 2:1**.

This is a picture of God's plan of salvation to set people free from earthly powers. In one broad stroke, God painted a picture of His power and Kingdom. Let all the earth hear and understand this prophecy. Daniel presented a perfect predictive picture of the coming Kingdom of God that Jesus ushered into this world at a later date.

" . . . the essence of prophecy is to give a clear witness for Jesus." (Revelation 19:10)

CHAPTER 11

Merry Christmas Everybody! (0 AD)

"I bring you good news that will bring great joy to all people. The Savior – yes, the Messiah, the Lord – has been born today in Bethlehem, the city of David!" (Luke 2:10-11)

LIKE WE HAVE DONE all our lives, let's pull the ribbon loose, tear off the wrappings, and open the gifts. This time it is a singular gift—Jesus, the Messiah, the Anointed One, the Christ, our Savior and Lord, the only Mediator between God and humans. "For there is only one God and one Mediator who can reconcile God and humanity—the man Christ Jesus. He gave his life to purchase freedom for everyone. This is the message God gave to the world at just the right time." **(1 Timothy 2:5-6)**

God did not give up on His plan to set us free from the devil's grip. The gift of Jesus would make that happen. That is why Christmas is the time of cheer. It brings us the good news that stuns the world and causes us to sit up and take notice of God's love for us. He will do whatever it takes to bring us back to Him again.

It took a miracle to accomplish God's desire. God worked a supernatural wonder so His Son could be born in this world: a miracle called the Immaculate Conception. "This is how Jesus the Messiah was born. His mother, Mary, was engaged to be married to Joseph. But before the marriage took place, while she was still a virgin, she became pregnant through the power of the Holy Spirit." **(Matthew 1:18)** The story of Jesus' birth is documented historically in **Luke 2:1-20.** Due to that story, we thank God every Christmas for giving us Jesus, His Son, as our indescribable gift.

Christmas

God created the heavens and earth
What was His creation worth?
It was free and God was pleased
Too soon it would be diseased.

The snake slithered down the tree
And asked Eve "You want to be free?"
Only one tree she was not to touch,
The temptation was just too much.

She ate fruit from the forbidden tree,
Adam too, but they were not set free.
They gave our nature of sinners,
Now we're losers, not winners.

Jesus came with a plan to win,
To rescue earth and peoples within.
Born in Bethlehem, a baby,
Conquered evil, and not with a "maybe."

Died, buried, rose, ascended, ruling,
Jesus, reason for the season, no fooling.
The babe died for the human race,
Believers caught in God's embrace.

He freed us from sin,
And gave each the win.
Life in heaven and earth
What creation is worth.

Merry Christmas everybody!
Jesus saves, not Santa, gifts or money;
The Babe in us forever remains
Hallelujah, the Lord our God omnipotent reigns!

Ren Vandesteeg, December 2016

We saw the beginning of God's plan, in which He prophesied that someone would come to destroy the devil for what he had done to Adam and Eve. (Genesis 3:15) Next, we learned that God promised a son to Abraham and he believed God that it would happen. The Lord took note of Abraham's faith and counted him as a righteous man because he believed Him. His son (a descendant) would eventually become Jesus the Messiah. (Galatians 3:16) Following that promise to Abraham, we learned that the Messiah would come from the tribe of Judah, and that promise is peppered throughout the Bible. (Genesis 49:10) Then we listened as God told Moses at the burning bush that His name was I AM. (Exodus 3:14) We understood that Jesus was the I AM when He told people " . . . I tell you the truth, before Abraham was even born, I AM!" (John 8:58) It is impossible to separate Jesus from God because of the name I AM. God revealed Himself in two unique ways as the I AM. One way was at the burning bush and then as Jesus the Messiah.

We went on to understand that the Messiah would not only come from the tribe of Judah, but within that tribe of David's throne, and His Kingdom would last forever. (2 Samuel 7:16)

After the Davidic promise, we learned two prophecies about God's plan to set people free.

The first, prophecy was a combination of promises in Jeremiah 29:11, Ephesians 1:10, and John 3:16. God promised an earthly home for Israel and an eternal home.

The second prophecy in Daniel 2 showed God would destroy all earthly kingdoms and replace them with His eternal Kingdom.

We see a progression in the plan regarding Jesus. God said that one person would come to this world to destroy the devil. (Genesis 3:15) He said that person would come from the Israeli tribe of Judah and David's royal line. (Genesis 49:10 and 2 Samuel 7:16) God finalized that part of His plan when the prophet Micah predicted the Messiah would be born in Bethlehem of the tribe of Judah. (Micah 5:2) That prophecy was fulfilled in Matthew 2:1. God sent His angel Gabriel to Mary, Jesus' mother, and told her, "You will . . . give birth to a son . . . name him Jesus . . . and his Kingdom will never end!" (Luke 1:31-33) God's angel told Joseph, Jesus' earthly father, " . . . you are to name Him Jesus, for he will save his people from their sins." (Matthew 1:21)

We have traced the central message from Eden to the original Christmas. He is indeed the main character in the Bible; it is all about Him.

The story below captures the life of Jesus on earth in a most unforgettable manner.

One Solitary Life

By Dr. James Allen Francis

Here is a man who was born of Jewish parents in an obscure village, the child of a peasant woman . . . He worked in a carpenter shop until He was thirty, and then for three years He was an itinerant preacher. He never wrote a book. He never held an office. He never owned a home. He never went to college. He never put His foot inside a big city. He never traveled two hundred miles from the place where He was born. He never did one of the things that usually accompany greatness. He had no credentials but Himself. He had nothing to do with the world except the naked power of His divine manhood. While still a young man, the tide of popular opinion turned against Him. His friends ran away. One of them denied Him. He was turned over to His enemies. He went through the mockery of a trial. He was nailed to a cross between two thieves. His executioners gambled for the only piece of property He had on earth while He was dying, and that was His coat. When He was dead He was taken down and laid in a borrowed grave through the pity of a friend.

Nineteen wide centuries have come and gone and today He is the centerpiece of the human race and the leader of the column of progress. All of the armies that ever marched, and all the navies that were ever built, and all the parliaments that ever sat, and all the kings that ever reigned, put together have not affected the life of man upon this earth as powerfully and profoundly as that one *Solitary Life*.[13]

That Life came to this world to save people from their sins. God made sure that both of Jesus' parents understood that truth when He sent His angel to tell them to name their son, Jesus. Why that very name? Because *Jesus* means "The Lord saves."[14]

CHAPTER 12

The King Blitzes His Enemies (0 AD – 33 AD)

"Jesus traveled throughout the region . . . announcing the Good News . . . healed every kind of disease and illness . . . demon-possessed or epileptic or paralyzed – he healed them all." (Matthew 4:23-24)

GOD LAUNCHED A BLITZKRIEG on His enemy, the devil. A blitz or blitzkrieg is a sudden, swift, vigorous, overwhelming barrage of power that attacks and defeats one's enemy.

God launched His lightning-fast attack on the devil and his evil forces through Jesus when He entered this world. It's as if Jesus parachuted in behind enemy lines. His presence on earth fired off an overwhelming, shock-and-awe volley of love and justice. Never before had one man defeated evil so devastatingly in such a short three-and-a-half-year period as Jesus did. The devil was in trouble.

Jesus, the King, came on the scene and invaded the devil's territory, bringing help to people, healing the sick, exposing and destroying the power of demons, and casting them out of people. Just as God promised. "For the Lord declares, 'I have placed my chosen king on the throne . . . I will give you the nations as your inheritance, the whole earth as your possession . . . what joy for all who take refuge in him!'" (Psalm 2:6, 8, 12)

The war God promised against satan was the onslaught that God started at Jesus' baptism. John the Baptist didn't want to baptize Jesus but Jesus said to him, "It should be done, for we must carry out all that God requires." **(Matthew 3:13 - 15)** Considering this, John baptized him. Immediately, two events took place: 1) the Holy Spirit descended on Jesus, and 2) God spoke audibly about Him to the crowd that had gathered to witness the baptism. " . . . as Jesus came up out of the water, the heavens were opened and he saw the Spirit of God descending like a dove and settling on him. And a voice from heaven said, 'This is my dearly loved Son, who brings me great joy.'" **(Matthew 3:16, 17)** Jesus allowed Himself to be baptized as an example for us to follow, in obedience to God our Father. When He did that humble act, the Holy Spirit came on Him to equip Him for the spiritual war that loomed ahead and the Father publicly put His stamp of approval on Jesus.

A military commander-in-chief (CINC, pronounced "sink") fully equips his handpicked soldier and publicly declares that he is his exclusive choice to lead his troops to victory. This is similar to what God did at Jesus' baptism. Jesus was the handpicked leader, designated by God the Father. You cannot be approved at a higher level than God Almighty, El-Shaddai. God gave Jesus total authority and power. This is how Father God showed the world that Jesus would be the one to execute His plan to set people free from the power of sin. Here again, we see God's heart. He sent the strongest being in the universe, His own Son, to destroy His archenemy and bring eternal life and freedom to frail humanity. Hail King Jesus!

Immediately after Jesus' baptism, the Holy Spirit led Him into the wilderness to be tempted by the devil. This was set up by God to defeat lucifer. **(Matthew 4:1-11)** Three times, the devil tempted Jesus by trying to get Him to do what he demanded. Each time, Jesus rebutted lucifer's temptations by saying, "It is written." You cannot go against God's book, the Bible, and win, as the devil found out. Jesus proved He was more powerful than lucifer when He used God's book as His offensive weapon. Jesus won that celestial boxing match by quoting scripture to His enemy. The devil tucked his proverbial tail between his legs and slinked off, sulking and looking for another opportunity to nail Jesus.

Through that temptation God lit the fuse to Jesus' ministry. He served notice that His Son would defeat satan in their spiritual war, as He predicted in Genesis. The temptation established the truth that Jesus had power over His archenemy even as He started His public ministry. The person God promised would come and destroy the devil was now on scene and humanity's Father immediately set up the showdown to prove His Son would destroy the enemy. The outcome would be certain. We can also say that Jesus established His authority over evil through this temptation event. He knew He came to this earth to defeat his enemy.

In Jesus' day, if a person or family was poor and needed welfare, they would appeal for help from a close relative who was called the *Goel*. The Hebrew word *Goel* comes from *lig'ol*, which means "to redeem."[15] The *Goel* was a redeemer for his kinsmen because he was responsible to restore the rights and avenge the wrong done to his relatives.

Jesus came as *our* Goel, to restore our rights and avenge the wrong done to us by the devil. He restores our rights by rescuing us from the devil's overwhelming power. He gives us eternal life and the freedom that satan took away. Our Goel avenges satan for the wrong he did to Adam and Eve in the garden and the hell he continues to do to us humans today. He will complete His vengeance when He appears at His second coming.

Now let's see our Goel in action during His first coming. The evangelist John Mark intensely described this tsunami of God's power, love, justice, and authority in *The Gospel of Mark*. We will look at this in the New King James Version because it captures this intensity best, especially with the word *immediately*. Mark chapter 1 sets the tone for Jesus' powerful ministry that lasted about forty-two months.

Here is a summary of Mark's first chapter. Let the blitz begin.

- Immediately, the Sprit descended upon Him.
- A voice came from heaven, "You are My Beloved Son."
- Jesus came . . . preaching . . . "Repent."
- Simon and Andrew . . . James and John . . . immediately . . . followed Him.
- Immediately on the Sabbath, He entered the synagogue and taught.
- They were astonished at His teaching, for He taught them as one having authority.
- Jesus rebuked him . . . "Be quiet, and come out of him!" The spirit came out.
- Immediately His fame spread throughout all the region.
- They brought to Him all who were sick . . . and demon-possessed.
- The whole city was gathered . . . He healed many who were sick . . . cast out demons.
- He said, "Let us go into the next towns, that I may preach there also."
- A leper came to Him . . . Jesus said . . . "be cleansed."
- Immediately, the leprosy left him . . . and they came to Him from every direction.

Jesus began His ministry when He said, "The time promised by God has come at last! The Kingdom of God is near. Repent of your sins and believe the Good News!" **(Mark 1:15)** The phrase, "the time promised by God" refers to Old Testament scriptures that promised the Messiah would come into this world. He is now on scene and establishes His leadership.

Rabbis in Jesus' day shared their wisdom and taught what they had learned from others. Jesus however, often said, "But *I* say." It was not uncommon for Him to set Himself apart from other Rabbis with His higher authority. This shocked people and drew their attention because no one other than the Messiah, God's mouthpiece, would have the audacity and authority to say, "But *I* say."

Matthew, one of Jesus' disciples, quoted Him: "Don't imagine that I came to bring peace to the earth! I came not to bring peace but a sword." (Matthew 10:34) For the devil and his demons, it's been hell to pay ever since. For the next 1,260 days, Jesus would regularly pummel them by His authority and power.

Remember that God said He would put everything under Jesus' authority? (Ephesians 1:10) He showed that authority when He disrupted the storm on the sea and said, "Peace, be still" . . . and the storm stopped immediately. (Mark 4:39)

A few hours later, He went into a cemetery and kicked out a legion of demons from a demon-possessed man who snapped chains from his wrists and smashed shackles when the government tried to control him. A legion was six thousand troops in the Roman Army of that day. Whether this man had six thousand demons in him is not the point. The point is, demons totally controlled him. No one could subdue him, but Jesus did. The legion of demons begged Jesus not to send them out of that region of the country, so He permitted them to go into a herd of pigs instead. (Mark 5:1-13)

Jesus invaded His enemy's territory; He took aim and commenced firing. He destroyed His enemies and set people free from the powerful grip those evil beings had on humans. People could experience the love, grace, and mercy of God when He set them free. Nothing would ever be the same again in the devil's lair on this earth.

When He began His ministry, Jesus went on the offensive and took His fight directly to the enemy. The warfare He unleashed was, and continues to be, the celestial spiritual war between Him and the devil. He unmasked the devil and his demons, disarmed them, and ultimately will cast them into the lake of fire (which we most commonly call hell). He will accomplish that goal at the end of time, when He returns to this earth—but we're getting ahead of ourselves.

How did Jesus take His fight to the enemy? "He canceled the record of the charges against us and took them away by nailing them to the cross. In this way, he disarmed the spiritual rulers and authorities. He shamed them publicly by his victory over them on the cross." (Colossians 2:14, 15)

Jesus defeated His enemies every time He forgave people of their sins, healed the sick, cast out demons, raised the dead, spoke the truth, and when He overwhelmed the smartest religious leaders and educated people with His wisdom. His entire ministry was an example of God's plan in action: when He destroyed His spiritual enemies, He set people free from them.

Jesus did not concern Himself only with His enemies. He also conducted business about the souls of people when He said, "And what do you benefit if you gain the whole world but lose your own soul? Is anything worth more than your soul?" (Mark 8:36-38) To wit, Jesus said, "Dear friends, don't be afraid of those who want to kill your body; they cannot do any more to you after that. But I'll tell you whom to fear. Fear God who has the power to kill you and then throw you into hell. He's the one to fear." (Luke 12:4, 5)

Jesus has power over souls. We need to be wise and live in awe of Him. We must show Him reverence and respect. Come to Him with a humble attitude and He will give us eternal life, the ultimate freedom.

Those around the world who believe in Him no longer need to fear the devil or death because Jesus set them free from satan. Jesus came, He conquered, He set believers* free in this life and the next.

God confirmed that Jesus was the One chosen to carry out His plan of salvation and freedom when He affirmed Jesus on the Mount of Transfiguration. (Luke 9:28-36) Peter, James, and John, three disciples who were with Jesus at the time, saw His preexistent glory shine through His physical body on that mountain when a cloud enveloped them and a voice said, "This is my Son, my Chosen One. Listen to him." (Luke 9:35) People need to heed this message if they want eternal life and freedom. *Listen to Him.*

Toward the end of His ministry, Jesus suffered for all the good He had done. This suffering is the next element in God's plan. In fact, suffering, along with Jesus' death, burial, and resurrection are the core to the entire plan for salvation and freedom. Here is how it worked. Jesus' head-on clash with evil cost Him His life. That was God's very plan from the beginning. Only when Jesus suffered, died, was buried, and rose from the dead, could He crush the head of the snake and destroy the devil—just as God perfectly predicted. (Genesis 3:15)

*Please note that I generally use the word *believer(s)* instead of *Christian(s)* to identify people who truly and actively believe, follow, and obey Jesus. I use this term because today's world has generally redefined the term *Christian* to mean *You're automatically a Christian if you're not an atheist, Buddhist, Islamic, Jew, Hindu, or a member of another religion.*

CHAPTER 13

The Blitz Interrupted (33 AD)

"He gave his life to purchase freedom for everyone." (1 Timothy 2:6)

JESUS' BLITZ CAME TO a screeching halt when the world crashed in on Him. The church in His day, His followers, friends, culture, and government rejected Him. For a long time, His enemies plotted to kill Him. Elite, religious people spread lies about Him, which the gullible public believed. They made matters worse when they joined in juicy gossip and spread truth-robbing rumors far and wide. The noose tightened around Him throughout the last week of His life until Thursday evening. That is when a former friend, Judas, betrayed Him to Roman soldiers, who promptly arrested Jesus and brought Him into custody.

Don't think these events took Jesus by surprise. Before His trials even began, Jesus confidently said He would defeat His archenemy. ". . . the ruler of this world approaches. He has no power over me . . ." (John 14:30) He followed that statement with this one: "I have told you all this so that you may have peace in me. Here on earth you will have many trials and sorrows. But take heart, because I have overcome the world." (John 16:33)

Jesus spoke those two statements *before* He suffered, was crucified, and died. It was as if He winked to His disciples with a knowing smile on His face. He reassured them that although all hell was about to break loose on Him, they should not worry. He had power and authority over the devil. Everything would be all right.

A small, powerful group of self-righteous religious leaders forced Jesus into the mockery of false trials in the church. They caused the Kangaroo Court to hand Him over to the Roman government for punishment. They wanted blood.

On Friday, governor Pilate weakly defended Jesus but eventually gave Him over to His accusers. They were powerful enough to talk their government into killing Jesus, even though He was innocent.

"Then Pilate had Jesus flogged with a lead-tipped whip. The soldiers wove a crown of thorns and put [pressed] it on his head and they put a purple robe on him. 'Hail! King of the Jews!' they mocked, as they slapped him across the face." **(John 19:1-3)** Religious people, along with government authorities, tortured Jesus physically, psychologically, and spiritually—body, soul, and spirit. The Jesus haters ridiculed Him, slapped Him, cut Him, whipped and beat Him within an inch of His life.

This was all according to God's plan. " . . . He was beaten so we could be whole. He was whipped so we could be healed . . . But it was the Lord's good plan to crush him and cause him grief. Yet when his life is made an offering for sin, he will have many descendants." **(Isaiah 53:5, 10)**

The next step in God's plan was to use the forces of darkness to crucify His son. Like we tenderize meat to prepare a meal, evil people pummeled Jesus. His back was whipped until it laid bare. On the street, called the Via Dolorosa, the crowd saw the muscles in His back, ligaments, tendons, cartilage exposed; and blood vessels bleeding life out of His body. Leaving a trail of blood behind Him, Jesus finally reached the top of Mount Calvary, called The Skull or Golgotha, ready to be crucified. "There they nailed him to the cross." **(John 19:18)**

Soldiers unmercifully forced Him, with His back open and bleeding, onto the rough, splintered beams of wood. They stretched out His aching and bruised arms and legs, and with masochistic delight, drove spikes into His hands and feet to secure Him to the cross. If that wasn't painful enough, the soldiers raised the head end of the cross, aimed the foot end into the waiting hole, and dropped it in. Thud! Jesus' raw, bleeding back slid down onto the sharp wooden slivers that protruded from the rough wood. The jolt when the cross hit the bottom of the hole would have been more than a body could take. But Jesus took it. He took it for you and me.

Jesus hung between heaven and earth. The Messiah came to mediate between God and sinful people and mediate He did. He took the sins of people for all of history onto Himself. He breathed His last when He said, "It is finished!" **(John 19:30)** Then He bowed His head and died.

He paid everyone's debt to God for being a sinner. Jesus, the Lion of the tribe of Judah, became the Lamb that was slain, slaughtered in our place. That is the meaning of the Crucifixion, the apex of God's plan for our salvation. The reprehensible deed was done.

The devil must have thought He had finally defeated his archenemy. Little did he know that Jesus' horrific death was part of God's plan all along. God planned for His Son to die. " . . . it was the Lord's good plan to crush him and cause him grief." (Isaiah 53:10)

"When he [God] sees all that is accomplished by his [Jesus] anguish, he [God] will be satisfied. And because of his experience, my righteous servant will make it possible for many to be counted righteous, for he will bear all their sins." (Isaiah 53:11) Jesus did not die a loser. Instead, He won a celestial victory. The prophet Isaiah nailed it when he said,

"I will give him the honors of a victorious soldier, because he exposed himself to death." (Isaiah 53:12)

Why did Jesus have to die as part of God's plan? "Because God's children are human beings – made of flesh and blood – the Son also became flesh and blood. For only as a human being could he die, and only by dying could he *break the power of the devil*, who had the power of death. Only in this way could he *set free* all who have lived their lives as slaves to the fear of dying." (emphasis mine; Hebrews 2:14-15)

How did God plan to break the devil's power? By dying on the cross, Jesus appeased (satisfied) God's wrath against us who are guilty of sin. By His death, Jesus turned God's wrath away from us and onto Himself, so instead of punishing us, God punished Jesus.

Therefore, all who believe Jesus died for them are free from punishment and eternal damnation. Once we put our faith in Jesus, we become children of God. In that transaction, God gave us the freedom He created in Adam and Eve. Before they sinned, they lived freely and in a right relationship with God. They were perfect. We live freely with God and in a right relationship with Him when we repent (feel remorse and change our minds about sin). We are not perfect but will be when we enter heaven.

From the moment we believe in Jesus, we enter God's freedom. Jesus set us free from lucifer's torturous bondage. In Jesus, we experience life filled with freedom, both now and in eternity; radically free in this life and the next.

The Christian hymn *I Will Sing of My Redeemer* captured the teaching on freedom in the first verse and chorus:

"I will sing of my Redeemer
And His wondrous love to me;
On the cruel cross, He suffered
From the curse to set me free.
Chorus

Sing, O sing of my Redeemer,
With His blood, He purchased me;
On the cross He sealed my pardon,
Paid the debt and made me free."[16]

But God's plan did not end with the Crucifixion.

The next facet of God's plan was the burial of Jesus' body. Late that Friday afternoon, after Jesus died, Joseph from Arimathea (with his friend Nicodemus) took Jesus down from the cross and laid Him in a tomb. "Following Jewish burial custom, they wrapped Jesus' body with the spices in long sheets of linen cloth." **(John 19:40)**

Jesus suffered, was crucified, died, and was buried on Friday (commonly called Good Friday in Christian churches). His body laid in the tomb until Sunday morning.

What happened to God's plan? Was Jesus' suffering, crucifixion, death, and burial the demise of His vision for restoring people? The devil must have thought so. Little did he know that God was not done with His plan.

CHAPTER 14

The Devil's Party
(33 AD)

"The place of crucifixion was near a garden, where there was a new tomb, never used before . . . they laid Jesus there." (John 19:41-42)

HOW LUCIFER AND HIS demons must have enjoyed Friday, watching Jesus lose His trial in a religious Kangaroo Court. They sadistically enjoyed watching Him as He agonized under the whipping of lead balls and hook-tipped ends pulverizing and ripping His flesh apart. The enemy watched Him stumble on His death march to Golgotha. They especially must have enjoyed His agony when the soldiers crucified Him. Their perverted pleasure felt luxurious as they watched Jesus die.

Satan's loss to Jesus when he tempted Him in the wilderness three and a half years earlier blazed again like white phosphorous lightning, blinding his arrogant, sadistic mind. He probably thought, "This time I've got you!" How smug he must have felt when he saw Jesus die. Total self-aggrandizement filled his dark soul while he watched Joseph and Nicodemus take Jesus' lifeless, bloody body down from the cross and lay it in the tomb.

Imagine lucifer's banquet hall that Friday evening as he entered to the delight of his cheering, demon army. They rose from their seats to applaud him as he strode to the head table. He stood at his chair, drinking in the adoration and adulation his narcissistic mind told him he so richly deserved. When the applause subsided, lucifer's director of staff raised his champagne glass, and with a shout, led his fellow demons in a toast to their leader.

"To you, oh mighty lucifer, our great potentate! To the chief!"

"To the chief!" the demons roared in chorus. Then sipping the champagne, each enjoyed the taste as they swirled the nectar in their mouths and swallowed.

Satan's chief of operations gave the next toast. "Congratulations boss, your plan worked perfectly!"

"Hear. Hear."

More booze down the hatch.

Next came the demon prince of the Middle East. "D-day in Israel sir. We won this battle. In a brief time, we will deceive and imprison everyone, just like you did in Eden. Bottoms up."

Glasses tipped during the last of the official toasts, as the alcohol slid down cursing throats. The demons reveled as they toasted each other, raising their champagne glasses in their gnarly, pointy-fingered hands for a job well done.

"Here's to you, my friend. Well done!"

"Thanks!"

"Here's to all you guys."

"And back at ya."

One demon tried to outdo the other. Humor, cynicism, and irony spurted from evil tongues as twisted minds gushed hate in a socially acceptable manner.

These were the same fallen angels who followed lucifer when he rebelled against God in heaven ages ago. They were still smarting about how the Creator unmercifully kicked them out of heaven and threw them down to the earth because they had rebelled against Him. (Revelation 12:7-9) Smarting or not, they were feeling pretty good at that point. They finally got their revenge! They killed God's one and only Son. What a prize!

For three horrible days, the devil and his army partied and celebrated their vile victory. Their archenemy was dead forever . . . or so they thought.

It was Friday . . . but Sunday was on its way!

CHAPTER 15

The King Returns
(33 AD)

"He is risen from the dead, just as he said would happen."
(Matthew 28:6)

THAT SUNDAY MORNING, HEAVEN'S Commander-in-Chief broke the dawn's early light with an earthquake. The very security that the Roman government of Caesar and Pilate counted on, the same secure ground that the hypocritical, elite religious leaders trusted in, trembled beneath their feet. An angel came to the tomb to roll the rock away. He opened death's door to the morning light. Brutal Roman soldiers were standing guard over the tomb and when they saw the angel coming, they fainted. Human toughness is no match for the presence of God.

God the Almighty had just performed the most important event in human history, while the prideful, political, military, and elite religious leaders slept. God interjected Himself into earthly history once again, but this time, He raised His Son from the dead.

Lucifer, turn out the lights. The party's over.

Attention! The funeral for Jesus has been canceled. We don't need a coffin or a cemetery. No need for an inurnment for ashes, a columbarium, or official mourners. Get that bunny and his Easter eggs out of here too. This is no place for a silly, scared rabbit. This is about the sacred Lamb. He is now the Lion of Judah who continues His assault on His enemies and sets captivated humanity free.

Now, let's trace God's plan through the three remaining events of Jesus' ministry while He was still on earth: His resurrection, the Great Commission, and His ascension.

The angel said " . . . 'He is risen' . . . 'I know you are looking for Jesus who was crucified. He isn't here! He is risen from the dead, just *as he said would happen* . . . '" (emphasis mine; **Matthew 28:5-6**)

Those three little words, "He is risen," are the pinnacle of human and universal history. Those words cement the greatest victory in the preeminent war ever fought—the spiritual war between God and the devil. The existence of the universe and the souls of humans hung in the balance as the prize for the victor. God defeated the devil and demonstrated His power over life *and death* when He ripped the power of death out of the devil's hands and raised Jesus from the dead. " . . . Christ was raised from the dead, and he will never die again. Death no longer has any power over him. When he died he died once to break the power of sin. But now that he lives, he lives to the glory of God." (Romans 6:9-10)

It was as if God announced to us, "I am God, I am the only one who has power over life and death. I gave life to my dead Son and raised Him back to life. Now you need to turn to Him, because just as I gave Him life after death, I have empowered Him to give you life after death. Turn to my Son in faith and He will give you freedom and eternal life with Me in heaven."

Why did God do this? Because He loves us with His agape love, that special love He has for people. It is not some sentimental, humanistic love; it is much more than that. God's agape love is "the greatest personal force in and beyond the universe, bringing rebirth and resurrection to mankind, restoring and recreating the human to the original purpose for which we were created."[17]

This love is embedded in the Greek word *agape*, "God's limitless, personal, relentless energy that moves to fulfill His original purpose in creating mankind, which is that we should be in His image and likeness."[18]

In our American language, we use the word love in many different contexts. It is difficult to distinguish sometimes which love a person is talking about without knowing the context. The Greek language is much more specific. Therefore, it is easier for folks to interpret what is meant.

The Greek word *philos* is that love which refers to friendship. From it we derive the word philanthropy, which is unselfish concern for other humans, often shown by donations of money, gifts, or time. We also have the word, Philadelphia, which means city of brotherly love.

When people talk about sexual, intimate, romantic love, they refer to *eros* love, which gives us words such as erotic and eroticism.

Family, or *storge,* love is care expressed between family members, such as parents for their children, a mother nursing her child, a dad playing with his kids, or siblings caring for each other.

All these loves are good and necessary for healthy human life. God gave all of them to us. For eternal life however, we must distinguish agape from the other three loves so we can understand God's love to us in a clearer manner. Agape love is between God and us, vertical if you will, from heaven down to earth. Philos love is between humans, horizontal on the face of this earth so to speak, not vertical from heaven to earth. One does not need to be a believer in Jesus to show philos or human love to another human being; this love is expressed every day by believing and non-believing people alike. The same principle holds true for storge and eros. People who do not believe in Jesus can still have strong, loving family relationships and sex.

Agape is unique to God. He shows this as saving love to the human race. Through Jesus, He set us free from evil so we can have life abundantly on earth and in heaven. God loves us so much that He will do whatever it takes (including killing His own Son) to gather us fallen and imprisoned people into His loving arms. What a love! That's not *amore,* that's *agape.*

When we have received that perfect freedom, we express agape love to others when we bring God into their lives. Any love we share with others that does not bring God to them for eternal life is not agape love. It can be philos (brotherly), eros (sexual), or storge (family) love. It is not agape if God's eternal salvation is not in it.

Often churches fail to realize this when they feed the poor or clothe the hungry but neglect to offer Jesus to them as their Savior and Lord. Any social not-for-profit organization can do good; it does not have to be a church. This is philos, humanistic love. The church should feed the hungry and help the poor, but more importantly it must present Jesus if it is a true church. Jesus said these cryptic words, "And what do you benefit if you gain the whole world but lose your own soul?" (Matthew 16:26)

We can gain warmth when we clothe the poor and stop hunger when we feed them, but what have we gained on their behalf if they do not hear the good news about Jesus? We must, as followers of Jesus, meet their greatest need, which is freedom and eternity with the Creator.

This is why Jesus coming to our world is the central message in the Bible. God directs His church to carry on His central message. He commands us to show God's eternal, saving, freeing, agape love to others so they can also be set free.

Even though death is still a part of our lives on earth, Jesus will extinguish mortality when He comes back at the end of time and ushers in eternity. "Then death and the grave were thrown into the lake of fire." (Revelation 20:14) Therefore, God's people never need to fear death again, in this life or the next. This is predicated on Jesus' resurrection.

Here's how it applies to us. Jesus paid for our guilt and sin when He was beaten, crucified, died, and laid in the tomb. When He rose from the dead, He defeated death and took authority over it. Therefore, He powerfully offers eternal life to you and me if we will accept it.

The power God used to raise Jesus from the dead is the same energy by which He gives us His eternal life. When we receive His life, we come alive spiritually. The first time we were born was physically. The second time we were born was spiritually. Therefore, we are "born again." It is that experience in which God uses His resurrection power to infuse His life into people. When we receive His life, we have life eternal.

The next facet in God's plan was to spread the good news of salvation and freedom to the world. Jesus planted the seed for this worldwide evangelistic movement when He told His disciples " . . . I have been given all authority in heaven and on earth. Therefore, go and make disciples of all the nations, baptizing them in the name of the Father and the Son and the Holy Spirit. Teach these new disciples to obey all the commands I have given you. And be sure of this: I am with you always, even to the end of the age." **(Matthew 28:18-20)**

We call these instructions from Jesus The Great Commission. Through this Commission Jesus continues God's plan to spread His good news to the world until He returns at the end of history.

The last element in Jesus' ministry while He was on earth was His ascension into heaven. This event came right after He gave His Great Commission. "Then Jesus led them to Bethany, and lifting his hands to heaven, he blessed them. While he was blessing them, he left them and was taken up to heaven. So, they worshiped him and then returned to Jerusalem filled with great joy." **(Luke 24:50-52)**

With the Great Commission ringing in their ears, Jesus left them and went up to heaven. He was gone, back to His throne, which He vacated thirty-three years earlier. His ascension was a critical step in God's plan for human salvation. Jesus had to return to His throne so He could equip His disciples, worldwide, to carry out the orders He gave them in the Great Commission. All of this was done to fulfill God's plan to set humans free from the devil, sin, evil, and eternal death.

Just as the wise men worshiped Jesus shortly after His birth, now His disciples worshiped Him as He returned to heaven. How fitting that Jesus' life was sandwiched between two bookends of worship. From the beginning of His life to the end, people worshipped Him because He is Immanuel, "God with us."

Let's summarize what we've learned about Jesus' ministry so far. God worked through Jesus *on earth*: blitzkrieg ministry, suffering, crucifixion, death, burial, resurrection, Great Commission, and ascension. These critical events in Jesus' life are the core to God's plan to set people free from evil.

In the next chapter, we will see the astounding truth of how God continued His work through Jesus. This time, Jesus will do His work *from heaven*. Jesus is still Immanuel, God with us, but in an entirely different manner.

CHAPTER 16

The King Resumes His Blitz (33 AD)

"But you will receive power when the Holy Spirit comes upon you. And you will be my witnesses, telling people about me everywhere . . . to the ends of the earth." (Acts 1:8)

JUST AS GOD BLITZED His enemy through Jesus while He was on earth, the Almighty planned to blitz the kingdom of evil again, but in a decisively different manner. From this point on, we will trace God setting people free through the power of the Holy Spirit in the church.

Jesus initiated His second blitzkrieg from the same throne room in which God planned His first blitz; therefore, heaven's throne room is once again the scene. The Bible refers to that room as heaven's court, the great assembly, the sanctuary, or the throne room.

I picture God's throne room to be a celestial version of a military command post. From that vantage point, God planned the Bible's central message of Him bringing freedom from evil to this world. It is from this Command and Control Center that Jesus calls, equips, and sends His people around the world to set people free from the ravages of corruption. Jesus did not travel the globe while He was on earth. In His entire lifetime, He never walked more than two hundred miles from His hometown. To carry out His clever plan, He would use other people's legs around the world to bring His good news globally.

The good news had to be brought because when Adam and Eve broke their relationship with God and disobeyed Him in the Garden of Eden they spawned their sinful nature and passed on their evil characteristics to humans all around the globe. That caused us to live sinfully and in broken relationships. Unless someone changed the course of that type of life, it would keep people around the world separated from God for eternity, and that is hell.

But God is love and He does not want us to live in a broken relationship with Him or to spend eternity in hell. In His agape love, He planned to fix that problem by sending Jesus to this world to pay for everything we messed up. "For God so loved the world that He gave His only begotten Son, that whoever believes in Him should not perish but have everlasting life." (John 3:16 NKJV)

When Jesus returned to His royal seat in heaven's throne room, He made good on His promise to His disciples, "But in fact, it is best for you that I go away, because if I don't, the Encourager won't come. If I do go away, then I will send him to you." (John 16:7)

Jesus lived on earth for forty days after He rose from the dead. Those are the forty days from Easter to Ascension Day. Ten days after His ascension, He executed the next action step in God's plan. That action step was Pentecost. If we add the forty days Jesus lived on earth after His resurrection to the ten days He was in heaven, we get a total of fifty days from Easter to Pentecost. The word *Penta* is Greek for fifty, so Pentecost is the fiftieth day after Jesus rose from the dead. On Pentecost, He carried out His promise in John 16:7 and baptized His Believers with His Holy Spirit. **(Acts 1:8)** Why did He do this? Why was Pentecost important in God's redemptive plan?

God the Father, God the Son, and God the Holy Spirit are the three persons that make God understandable to us. Theologians call this the Trinity. Another word they use is Triune, meaning three in one. This means that the one and only God reveals Himself to humans through three persons—the Father, the Son, and the Holy Spirit. Without delving into a deep study of the Trinity, let's learn from God how He put together the remainder of His plan.

Have you ever sat in the public gallery of your state capitol or the nation's Capitol in Washington D.C. and watched government officials, senators, and representatives conduct their work? Have you ever observed a judge or panel of judges as they settled a case? Imagine that we are inside heaven's throne room. There sit the three persons of the Trinity—Father, Jesus, and Holy Spirit. Father sits in the middle chair, Jesus sits to Father's right, (which is the place of authority and power), and Holy Spirit sits to Father's left. Jesus has just returned from His thirty-three years on earth and reunited with His Father and the Holy Spirit. They have the remainder of their plan laid out on the table in front of them. They are ready to execute the next step in their blitz to win the universal, spiritual war against their enemies: the world, the flesh, and the devil (also known as governments, immorality, and evil).

The next action step in God's plan was to send the Holy Spirit to our world. Just as the Father sent Jesus here at Christmastime, thirty-three years earlier, to blitz the enemy and bring the good news of God's Kingdom, now it would be the Holy Spirit's turn. As a spirit, He could go around the globe and move on hundreds, thousands, millions, or billions of people's hearts simultaneously, so people could be set free and believe in Jesus for eternal freedom. This is what Jesus, the individual Rabbi, could not do globally. But the Holy Spirit could. This would become blitzkrieg number two.

"H hour" has arrived. "H" hour is the exact moment when a military commander executes his plan of attack. That's precisely what the Father did when He sent the Holy Spirit to this earth. Look at the following scriptures in which Jesus told His disciples, before He was crucified, that the Father would send the Holy Spirit to His followers.

" . . . he will give you another Advocate, who will never leave you. He is the Holy Spirit, who leads into all truth. (John 14:16-17)

"When the Spirit of truth comes, he will guide you into all truth." (John 16:13) Jesus told His disciples this good news in His farewell speech at suppertime on Thursday evening, the night before He was murdered fifty-three days earlier.

After He rose from the dead, Jesus added this, " . . . do not leave Jerusalem until the Father sends you the gift he promised, as I told you before . . . you will be baptized with the Holy Spirit." (Acts 1:4, 5)

Enter the Holy Spirit. Acts 2 described this phase in God's freedom plan when He launched the Pentecostal blitz into world history. On Pentecost, earth's history entered the era of Holy Spirit leadership. Our world would never be the same again.

CHAPTER 17

Pentecost
(33 AD)

"On Pentecost . . . there was a sound from heaven . . . it filled the house . . . what looked like flames or tongues of fire . . . settled on each of them." (Acts 2:1 - 3)

IN ACTS 2 JESUS baptized believers with His Holy Spirit on Pentecost in Jerusalem, ten days after He ascended to heaven. The Holy Spirit surprised everyone when He gave believers the ability to tell the good news about Jesus in languages they had never spoken. The purpose of this gift of tongues was to make it easy for people to hear the good news about Jesus in their own language.

"Suddenly, there was a sound from heaven like the roaring of a mighty windstorm . . . it filled the house . . . flames or tongues of fire appeared and settled on each of them [about 120 people] . . . And everyone present was filled with the Holy Spirit . . . speaking in other languages as the Holy Spirit gave them this ability." (Acts 2:2 - 4) For example, Matthew, one of Jesus' disciples may have told Arabians about Jesus in their language, even though he never spoke Arabian before.

People from all over the world were in Jerusalem at the time and rushed to the scene when they heard the loud noise of something like a raw, high-gust windstorm. Due to the blasting winds, they had to shout louder than the noise so they could hear each other. They said, ". . . we all hear these people speaking in our own languages about the wonderful things God has done!" (Acts 2:11)

Indeed, God was doing a new thing, something no one expected. He spoke through the prophet Joel (approximately 830 years earlier) that He would pour out His Spirit on all people. Joel had perfectly predicted that "sons and daughters would prophesy, young men would see visions, and older men would dream dreams." **(Joel 2:28-32)** God would pour out His Spirit on servants, men and women alike, and everyone who called on the name of the Lord would be saved. That day arrived on Pentecost. **(Acts 2:16-18)**

Ten days earlier, Jesus commissioned His disciples to go into the world to tell people about Him. This event on Pentecost was the first step in that commission. His followers obeyed and told the worldwide crowd about Jesus. A good example is what Peter said, "People of Israel, listen! God publicly endorsed Jesus the Nazarene by doing powerful miracles, wonders, and signs through him, as you well know. But God knew what would happen, and his prearranged plan was carried out . . . " (Acts 2:22-23)

Peter boldly referred to God's redemptive plan when he said it was a prearranged plan. We have traced that plan to this point and saw how God prearranged Jesus' betrayal, suffering, death, burial, and resurrection. But who would have thought He also prearranged the start of the Great Commission this way?

Indeed, God prearranged His good news to go worldwide and He accomplished that on Pentecost. When the crowd dispersed and returned to their homes throughout the world the following week, they spread the good news to their families and friends. In this manner, God, as Holy Spirit, brought the message to the world starting on Pentecost.

In addition to introducing tongues that day for instant worldwide evangelism, the Holy Spirit added a second surprise when He launched the church—that group of people who believed in Jesus. We could call Pentecost the birthday of the church. On this special day, God ushered two eras into world history: the era of the Holy Spirit and the era of the church. These two converged on Pentecost and started the next phase in God's redemptive plan.

The Holy Spirit and the church are inseparable for the rest of human history as they carry out the Great Commission together, like a hand in a glove. The Holy Spirit continues the blitzkrieg Jesus started three and a half years earlier. He does it through the church.

The Holy Spirit has a specific purpose for His church, which is to tell people about the wonderful things God has done. The most wonderful thing God did was to bring Jesus into this world to set humanity free from the devil's rule. It is the church's responsibility to proclaim that message to the world. It is called *The Missio Dei*, which means "God's Mission." It is His mission to share the Bible's central message of salvation with the world, and His tool to accomplish that is His church. I am a member of that church, and if you are also, then God's Mission, His *Missio Dei,* is *our* mission. We are God's megaphones to the world.

On Pentecost, the Holy Spirit initiated the church's responsibility to carry that great mission to the world. This started when the Holy Spirit led the church to invade the devil's territory by enabling her to speak in other tongues about the wonderful things God had done. As members of the church spoke, the church plundered the enemy's forces. They broke the power of evil spirits that held people in bondage to sin. Many in the crowd were led to believe in Jesus through the presentation of the gospel that day. The blitz continued. Welcome to the era of the Holy Spirit and the church.

To spread the good news globally would be a gargantuan job. Jesus and the Holy Spirit knew this. That was why the Messiah told his disciples " . . . apart from me you can do nothing." (John 15:5) He knew His people would need His help if they were to successfully bring the good news of salvation to the world. Under His Father's direction, He sent His Spirit as their helper, to lead, guide, and equip them.

When the Holy Spirit came to this earth at Jerusalem, He did not come to our world as some sort of objective force. Believers do not say, "May the force be with you." Instead they say, "May the source be with you." The Holy Spirit came on Pentecost as a person. He lives inside the bodies of humans who believe in and follow Jesus Christ.

He made His home in the believer's heart—not the blood pump, but the center of a human being that we call our heart, which is made up of our soul and spirit. Our soul is made up by our mind, will, and emotions. Our spirit is made up by our intuition, conscience, and communion with God. These elements make up our heart.

It was a miracle when the Holy Spirit came into believers' hearts on Pentecost. The supernatural, Almighty God who created us, chose to live inside our natural, mortal bodies. He has continued to do that ever since Pentecost. After He makes His home inside the believer, God the Holy Spirit helps, leads, guides, directs, equips, and empowers each follower for his or her kingdom work.

As the Holy Spirit filled each believer on Pentecost, He thereby filled the church also. We can turn that around and say that the church was Spirit-filled because the Holy Spirit filled each believer in that church. This is critical to understand. It is only the Spirit-filled church that will accomplish the Great Commission and fulfill God's plan through Spirit-filled believers—those who trust and obey Jesus.

When the Holy Spirit lives inside people, big surprises happen. The Holy Spirit gave us a glimpse of His power when He inspired the apostle Peter to preach on that Pentecost Sunday. People from around the world listened with rapt attention. This resulted in about three thousand believers added to the church that day. (Acts 2:41) Not bad for the first day that the Holy Spirit came inside humans and blitzed the enemy through one man's sermon.

After Peter preached his sermon, the Holy Spirit continued His blitz on the enemy by becoming personal, real personal, with His believers.

CHAPTER 18

Let's Get Personal (33 AD)

"And everyone present was filled with the Holy Spirit . . ." (Acts 2:4)

UP TO THIS POINT, we have studied and traced God's entire plan objectively, as if God was apart from us, outside of us, as if He and His plan were objects that we could study in seminary, Bible college, in a textbook, or under a microscope.

In this chapter, we will switch gears from an objective to subjective study, because God switched these gears in His plan. To keep up with Him, we will have to become personal with Him, as He does with us. We will study God and His plan subjectively as we look at our Savior from a more personal perspective, because the Holy Spirit resides in each believer since He arrived on earth on Pentecost. He continues to do so right up to our day and until Jesus returns at the end of time.

From now on, I will write as a member of His church in whom the Holy Spirit lives. If you believe in Jesus as Savior and Lord, we are in this together. If you are not a believer, I invite you to come along to observe how the Holy Spirit operates in the lives of believers. Hopefully, you will join us in faith at some point.

You become a believer by repenting of your sins (changing your mind about sin), asking God to forgive you of those sins, and receiving Jesus as the one God sent to set you free. If you do that, you are a believer. Welcome to the family of God.

God, the Holy Spirit, came into us when we first believed in Jesus as our Savior and Lord. From that moment on, He changed our very nature because He transformed us into new people. "This means that anyone who belongs to Christ has become a new person. The old life is gone; a new life has begun!" (2 Corinthians 5:17) We, then, become more personal with God because He renewed us into His image so that we become like Him. Our spirit now

> " . . . contains the DNA of the divine . . . We are no longer limited to live by the dictates of our . . . natural mind. We are like a bird let out of a cage, set free to soar. Every force that would confine us is broken, and we are powerfully reborn with the nature of our Father on the inside of us. We are . . . created to move and dwell in the Spirit, unlocking limitless possibilities."[19]

Limitless possibilities for us? Really? Jesus made this possible when He started something new. In the Old Testament (the old covenant), the Holy Spirit came upon certain individuals at specific times. In the New Testament, He came to live *in* and *stay in* believers. We believers do not have only an occasional taste of God, but a continual feast of His Spirit and life within our lives.

In this new covenant, God relates to us as the new people He made us to be. He guides us through our human spirit by His Holy Spirit inside of us. Jesus steers us away from sin and into a new life of radical freedom and liberty in God. We fulfill the purpose for which we were created, which was to mirror God to others, worship Him, and live in close relationship with Him. "Bring all who claim me as their God, for I have made them for my glory. It was I who created them." (Isaiah 43:7)

With God residing in us, we understand that our relationship with Him is personal and we live in freedom: "For the Lord is the Spirit and wherever the Spirit of the Lord is, there is freedom." (2 Corinthians 3:17) We are walking examples of the Bible's central message.

We will study the remainder of God's plan from the perspective that we are absolutely free people. We *image* Him by mirroring Him to the world through His special agape love. Therefore, from now on, we will study God's freedom plan subjectively, experiencing God, the Holy Spirit, and His freedom along the way as we become intimate and personal with Him and He with us. We cannot see the Holy Spirit, but we can experience Him.

Since the Holy Spirit is a person, I will now drop the word "the" before His name and will simply call Him—Holy Spirit. We call Jesus by His name. We do not call Him, "the Jesus." We can call Holy Spirit by His name. Therefore, in the remainder of this book I will address Him as Holy Spirit, not "the" Holy Spirit (unless quoting from other sources).

Holy Spirit is our leader. I invite you to compare how the New Testament believers followed His leadership with how twenty-first century believers follow Him.

We note two patterns of action Holy Spirit shows in everything He does. First, He brings our attention to Jesus, not to Himself. Second, He works in harmony with the Bible. He never contradicts what He inspired men to write in the scriptures. The Bible is His book. He breathed His words into men as they wrote the Holy Book. That is why we call the Bible the inspired Word of God.

We will chronologically trace His actions. We begin at Creation. "In the beginning God created the heavens and the earth. The earth was formless and empty, and darkness covered the deep waters. And the *Spirit of God* was hovering over the surface of the waters." (emphasis mine; Genesis 1:1-2) Here we see Holy Spirit involved in creating the universe. Since the cosmos is His creation along with our Father and Jesus, He also redeems His once perfect creation and His people within it.

Throughout the Old Testament Holy Spirit came upon people to lead them to a specific action. "At that time, the Spirit of the Lord came upon Jephthah." (Judges 11:29) "And the Spirit of the Lord came powerfully upon David from that day on." (1 Samuel 16:13)

Now we leapfrog to the New Testament. In the book of Matthew, we read, " [Mary] . . . became pregnant through the power of the Holy Ghost." (Matthew 1:18) Holy Spirit supernaturally performed the Immaculate Conception, causing the Virgin Mary to conceive and become pregnant with Jesus. Throughout Old Testament history, God predicted He would send the Messiah to our broken world. To make that happen, Jesus would have to be born a human. God made that possible when Mary became pregnant by the power of Holy Spirit. Then Mary birthed Jesus into this world, and with her husband, Joseph, raised Him to adulthood.

At the age of thirty Jesus began His ministry, which lasted about three and a half years. He concluded His earthly ministry at His ascension when He told His disciples, " . . . you will receive power when Holy Spirit comes upon you. And you will be my witnesses . . ." (Acts 1:8) We see Holy Spirit at work in Jesus' life from His birth to His ascension.

Let's observe Holy Spirit as if we are watching Him in a movie, performing His work right before our eyes. God is eternally present, hence His name, I AM. This puts Holy Spirit into the present tense, which helps us to immediately know, understand, and apply Him to our lives.

"Attention on the set. Lights. Camera. Action!"

We pick up the action at Pentecost. Holy Spirit leaves heaven's throne room and appears in Jerusalem, but something is drastically different.

On Pentecost, God increases the momentum of His plan to set humans free when Holy Spirit effortlessly soars into our world in high velocity. He does not announce Himself and has everything under control. He immediately captures everyone's attention when, true to His character, He prompts His followers to tell the worldwide crowd in multiple languages about Jesus.

He makes it easy on the speakers. All they must do is speak and the appropriate language comes. Likewise, He makes it easy on the listeners. All they have to do is listen. They will hear their own languages. Then, Holy Spirit ends the day by supernaturally adding some three thousand people to the newly formed church. (Acts 2:41) Only Holy Spirit can pull this off.

In one day, God initiates His *Missio Dei*, His worldwide plan to set us free. He shifts His plan into high gear when Holy Spirit implements the Great Commission. Shake hands with blitzkrieg number two.

Pentecost begins the *last days*, the end-time stage in world history, between Jesus' ascension and His return to this world. In this era, Holy Spirit becomes personal with each believer. In us He defeats His enemies (the world, the flesh, the devil) by setting us free from their evil tyranny and gives us revolutionary freedom in our Spirit-filled lives.

He gives freedom not only for our good but to enable us to agape-love others who need God in their lives. In our freedom, we follow Holy Spirit's leading to bring restoration to others. This is our time to destroy spiritual enemies by setting people free in Holy Spirit's power.

The early church believers swiftly obeyed Holy Spirit when He sent them to set others free. Will we swiftly obey Him when He nudges us to set others free?

CHAPTER 19

Swift Obedience
(33 AD)

"Those who believed . . . were baptized and added to the church that day . . ." (Acts 2:41)

WHEN THE WORLD'S PEOPLE heard the gospel on Pentecost in their own languages they asked Peter, "what should we do?" He answered, " . . . Each of you must repent of your sins and turn to God . . ." (Acts 2:37 - 39) Peter answered with the same teaching Jesus used to start His ministry three and a half years earlier—*repentance*. Jesus began His blitzkrieg with, " . . . Repent of your sins and believe the Good News!" (Mark 1:15)

The Almighty, in His wisdom, started both blitzes the same way; with a call to repentance.

Why?

When we repent, God sets us free from our imprisonment to sin and bondage. The Greek word for repentance is *metanoia*, which literally means to *feel remorse and change one's mind*. To repent of sin means to change our minds along with a sense of remorse about our sins. God sees this as a must-do for any human to enter His Kingdom.

When we change our minds about sin, God gives us salvation. When we switch our thinking from bad to good, God releases us from the devil's grip. This release sets us free so we can live completely in God's love and power.

Peter experienced repentance and knew its absolute freedom. He wanted the same for the crowd when he saw their angst. He told them to repent and turn to God. Swiftly, thousands did. Swift obedience was apparently a characteristic of the early believers, because we see this trait permeated the early church.

God is an equal opportunity employer, so to speak. He gave Holy Spirit not only to the earliest believing Jews, but also to believing Gentiles, who were non-Jewish people from around the world. "God knows people's hearts and he confirmed that he accepts Gentiles by giving them the Holy Spirit, just as he did to us [Jews]." **(Acts 15:8)**

This includes all nations and ethnic groups around our globe throughout history. God loves the human race. After all, He created us equally and gives His agape love to each and every one of us without discrimination. This teaching kills off the evil of today's racism that holds one race as superior or inferior to another.

"There is no way to understand the cultural cancer of racism until we seriously read the Bible. For this breathtaking collection of 66 books is completely silent on our modern concept of 'races.' Tragically, blacks, Orientals, whites—all of us—have been pushed into 'boxes' (the metaphor of which is the stinking, grisly railroad car…of the Holocaust) and we have forgotten that God has 'made of one blood all nations of men.'" (Acts 17:26)[20]

God shows His equalizing love to *all* humans in this awesome verse, "But to all who believed him and accepted him, he gave the right to become children of God." **(John 1:12)**

The result for all who become children of God? "There is no longer Jew or Gentile, slave or free, male and female. For you are all one in Christ Jesus." (Galatians 3:28)

We are not all evangelists, but if we belong to Jesus and have Holy Spirit living inside of us, we are able to obey Him in whatever He directs us to do. This is intensely personal, which makes our swift obedience a key element as we participate in God's plan.

Holy Spirit " . . . is given by God to those who obey him." (Acts 5:32) That puts a premium on swift obedience for every believer who wants Holy Spirit in his or her life. If we have an intimate relationship with Jesus through Holy Spirit, we *desire* to obey Him. Obedience is no longer a chore. Through Holy Spirit, Jesus declares war on dead religion and we realize we don't *have* to obey, we *want* to.

When we obey, God responds and brings results. When we see those results we immediately understand that our obedience played a part in what God did. That enthuses us to obey even more. We do not obey to obtain results. We obey because it is fulfilling, gratifying, and God-glorifying.

Think about a love relationship between a husband and wife. He feels fulfilled when he gives her a dozen roses. He experiences her reactions of joy, a smile, a hug, a kiss, and wants to give her more flowers. He does not do this only to get more reaction from his wife; he continues to give her flowers and possibly more and bigger gifts because his love in action is a natural part of his intimate relationship with her. The more he does for her, the better he feels. That builds a strong marriage.

A strong, intimate, loving relationship must exist between Holy Spirit and us. The more we give of ourselves in obedience to Him, the better we feel and the more we accomplish. This cements our relationship and becomes a lifestyle for all who are intimately personal with Holy Spirit.

Holy Spirit always initiates the action when He wants us to do something. When He gives you a directive, do not worry if you think you cannot do it or do not have a clue how to do it. He will not give you a command you cannot obey.

He did not direct early believers to do something they were incapable of doing or set them up to fail. He does not change. He will work with you and me in the same way He did thousands of years ago. Let's learn how He did this by looking at three examples in which He started an action and then told a believer what to do next. Note the swift obedience.

1. Holy Spirit told Philip to go down a particular road. (Acts 8:26-40) No explanation, just, "Go." Philip did. Then, Holy Spirit told him to walk next to a carriage, which he did. He then met the treasurer of Ethiopia sitting in the carriage reading the Bible, but he did not understand it. Philip explained the scripture he was reading and "told him the good news about Jesus." (Acts 8:35) Then he baptized him and the treasurer went on to Ethiopia rejoicing; a very happy and fulfilled man of God.

2. Holy Spirit told Peter to go with three men to the house of Cornelius, a military officer. (Acts 10:19-20) He went and preached Jesus to him and the group that was gathered in his home. While he spoke, Holy Spirit fell on all who were listening. Afterwards, Peter baptized them.

3. Holy Spirit told the disciples to "Dedicate Barnabas and Saul for the special work to which I have called them." (Acts 13:2-3) The men laid their hands on them and sent them on their way. They sailed to Cyprus and ended up leading the island's governor to the Lord.

All three examples are simple and basic. Yet it is so profound when God comes into lives and prompts us to action. In these examples, Philip, Peter, and Saul with Barnabas, obeyed and did what they were told. That is the easy part. As we saw above, God will not tell you to do something He will not equip you to do. The hard part was left for Holy Spirit, which was to convert the listeners to God. That was no problem for Him, yet He chose not to do it in a vacuum. He employed willing believers who swiftly responded to His nudges and they told others about Jesus. Then, He worked in the hearts of the listeners, causing them to believe. We do not convert anybody. Holy Spirit does.

In these examples, Holy Spirit chose individuals who lived intimately with Him. He knew their hearts. They were tight with Him and He with them. Therefore, they swiftly obeyed Him. This same principle applies to us.

This gives us a good baseline from which to work and establish ourselves in God's plan. He gives us the honor and privilege to be involved in His central message. If we are personal with Holy Spirit, we will be swift to obey and accomplish His plan in our time.

CHAPTER 20

The King Blitzes the Middle East and Europe (33 – 95 AD)

"Therefore, go and make disciples of all the nations . . ."
(Matthew 28:18)

IN THIS CHAPTER, WE will continue to track God's message of freedom by following Holy Spirit through the remainder of the New Testament. We will see Him blitzing the Middle East and Europe in the books of Romans through Revelation. He inspired men to write books or letters to instruct believers how to live their Christian lives in freedom. That teaching established the early church to live a new lifestyle of freedom as people swiftly obeyed the instructions in those letters.

The apostle Paul wrote: "Sin is no longer your master . . . Instead, you live under the freedom of God's grace." (Romans 6:14)

Paul also wrote, "God has united you with Christ Jesus . . . he freed us from sin." (1 Corinthians 1:30) Whatever form of sin we have in our lives, we are set free from it and do not need to bow to its power any longer.

Is not God, Holy Spirit, in each believer? Of course. That's where His freedom is—in you. "For the Lord is the Spirit, and wherever the Spirit of the Lord is, there is freedom." (2 Corinthians 3:17) Therefore, wherever you are, you live in freedom because the Spirit of the Lord is in you.

God continues to flood us with good news on the topic of freedom: "You are trying to earn favor with God by observing certain days or months or seasons or years . . . I plead with you to live as I do in freedom from these things, for I have become like you . . . free from those laws." (Galatians 4:10-12)

In the book of Colossians God also teaches us freedom on a higher level: "You have died with Christ, and he has set you free from the spiritual powers of this world. So why do you keep on following the rules of the world . . .?" (Colossians 2:20-21) The spiritual powers of this world that Paul refers to include religious restrictions, such as living a life of asceticism, or extreme denial of legitimate needs. In Christ, we are free to follow Him. We do not need to go to any extremes to win God's favor. Believers already have God's favor. He gave us His eternal freedom out of His grace, not because of our behavior.

Paul told Timothy, "Through the power of the Holy Spirit who lives within us, carefully guard the precious truth that has been entrusted to you." (2 Timothy 1:14) That truth refers to the central message in the Bible, which is Jesus, who came to this world to set us free.

No book makes a better case for swiftly following the freedom of Jesus Christ than the book of Hebrews. "This is the new covenant I will make with my people on that day, says the Lord . . . I will never again remember their sins and lawless deeds." (Hebrews 10:16-17) There is no freer way to live as a believer than to know God will never again remember our sins. We are forever free from them.

Peter taught that the salvation the prophets preached was for us. (1 Peter 1:11-16) We are now to look forward to the salvation that will come when Jesus is revealed to the world. To look forward becomes our focus and anticipation of the complete freedom we will receive when Jesus comes at the end of time. The anticipation keeps us strong in the Lord and causes us to live as God's obedient children, who do not slip back into our old ways. Instead, we live as holy people in freedom because Holy Spirit lives in us.

Holy Spirit provided strong teaching in the book of Jude. He prompted Jude, one of Jesus' brothers, to write against the false teaching that had crept into the church in his day. The false teaching said that God is gracious; therefore, believers could live immoral lives. Nothing could be further from the truth. "So, I want to remind you, though you already know these things, that Jesus first rescued the nation of Israel from Egypt, but later he destroyed those who did not remain faithful." (Jude 5)

Those are tough words, but Holy Spirit knew the early church needed to hear His teaching. He then encouraged the early church, "But you, dear friends, must build each other up in your most holy faith, pray in the power of the Holy Spirit, and await the mercy of our Lord Jesus Christ, who will bring you eternal life. In this way, you will keep yourselves safe in God's love." (Jude 20) Being safe in God's love is the place of freedom.

Holy Spirit confirmed this safety in the book of Revelation. While John worshiped in the Spirit, Jesus told him to write the book of Revelation. (Revelation 1:10-11) Holy Spirit was the portal through whom Jesus spoke to inspire John to write Revelation. From this, we understand that Holy Spirit has His fingerprints all over the book of the end times as He brings the central message of salvation to a climax. "He who is the faithful witness to all these things says, 'Yes, I am coming soon!'" (Revelation 22:20-21) The one in whom we believers are safe is coming soon to usher us into eternity, our ultimate freedom. Maranatha! Come quickly, Jesus!

This concludes our whirlwind tour with Holy Spirit through the New Testament. Throughout it, Holy Spirit brought Jesus to the Middle East, Rome, Italy, and Europe. Throughout history, He takes Jesus to the rest of the world and continues the Great Commission right up to the end when the Messiah will return.

CHAPTER 21

The King Lives in Believers (61 AD - Present)

"Christ lives in you." (Colossians 1:27)

JESUS HAS NOT RETURNED yet. Therefore, the instructions Holy Spirit gave believers from 33 AD to 95 AD pertain all the way to us in the twenty-first century. As God blazed His plan through the Middle East and Europe over two thousand years ago, His firestorm continues today. His central message dealt with believers then, and it deals with believers now. Through Holy Spirit, Jesus came to live in New Testament Christians and all believers throughout history.

" . . . Christ lives in you . . . " **(Colossians 1:27)** Jesus, the Christ, came into us by His Holy Spirit when we first believed in Him. He decided to stay the rest of our lives. "And because we are his children, God has sent the Spirit of his Son into our hearts." (Galatians 4:6)

He leads us by His Spirit, just as He led believers in biblical times. If we follow Him as the early church did, Holy Spirit will teach us how we fit into God's plan.

When we became a part of that plan, God gave us the responsibility to spread the good news to the world, just as He directed the New

Testament church. When He gave us His Spirit to help us bring the gospel of freedom to the world, He also gave us a bonus, so to speak: Holy Spirit fills our hearts with God's love. " . . . We know how dearly God loves us, because he has given us the Holy Spirit to fill our hearts with his love." (Romans 5:5) That love is agape.

With agape love, He motivates us to go into the world and distribute the good news about Jesus the Messiah. I use the word *distribute* instead of *tell* because telling is only one way to spread the good news of Jesus. We are not all good "tellers." But we can distribute the good news in ways that fit our personalities, character traits, likes and dislikes, and work environments.

For example, a professional truck driver can talk about Jesus in a conversation at a truck stop quite easily because that is his environment. He is comfortable with other haulers and wild-catters. They would be relaxed with him and more apt to receive his witness to Christ. A rocket scientist, a farmer, a CEO, an hourly wage earner, a doctor, a recovering drug addict, a Silicon Valley executive, or a million others, are more apt to distribute Jesus or believe in Him in their work environment. In this way, we are involved in God's plan to set people free and we exercise our responsibility to keep His plan going. God blesses us with fulfillment and success in other areas of our lives while we bring Jesus to others.

To distribute the good news of Jesus we must be physically fit. We must honor God with our physical bodies. "Don't you realize that your body is the temple of the Holy Spirit, who lives in you and was given to you by God? You do not belong to yourself, for God bought you with a high price. So, you must honor God with your body." (1 Corinthians 6:19-20)

We honor God with our bodies by taking care of our physical flesh, so that we can give Him the best possible house in which to live. Quite literally, this is "Christ *in* you." (Colossians 1:27) If He comes to live in us, it stands to reason that we believers must give Him the best home (body) we can, out of reverence and respect for Him.

When I was on faculty at the U.S. Air Force Chaplain School, my area of responsibility was to teach and train chaplains how to prepare for deployment to hot spots around the world or how to minister in wartime conditions. I taught my students, "You have to take care of yourself. You cannot do ministry if you are dead." We take care of our bodies by eating and drinking healthy food, exercising, staying sexually pure, having enough rest, and watching our weight. In this way, each believer honors God in his or her body, stays healthy, and is physically able to communicate Jesus to a dying world. After all, we are the temples of Holy Spirit. "Don't you realize that your body is the temple of the Holy Spirit, who lives in you [singular] and was given to you by God? You do not belong to yourself, for God bought you with a high price. So, you must honor God with your Body." (1 Corinthians 6:19)

But Holy Spirit does not live only in our individual physical bodies. He also lives corporately in the Body of Christ, which we call the church. "Don't you realize that all of you together are the temple of God and that the Spirit of God lives in you?" (1 Corinthians 3:16)

In addition to taking care of our physical bodies, believers are responsible to take care of our spiritual body—the church. Believers do this by caring for each other. Healthy churches, made up of spiritually healthy believers, bring God's freedom to the world. "We prove ourselves by our purity . . . by the Holy Spirit . . . God's power is working in us." (2 Corinthians 6:6-10)

What if we get off track? We may sin, make a mistake, or become tired and mess things up. Then what?

We return to Holy Spirit. " . . . to be filled with the Holy Spirit." (Ephesians 5:18) The verb, "to be filled," is in the present-progressive tense. Therefore, it means "to be *continually* filled." Believers accomplish this by living intimately with Holy Spirit. When we mess up, we need to return to Holy Spirit, His presence, His agape love, and His power. We are filled in this manner many times in our faith walk. The New Testament believers were filled with Holy Spirit several times, which was apparently a common experience. It's not any different for us.

For example, Jesus baptized the Ephesian Christians with His Holy Spirit in Acts chapter 19. Yet, later, they were told to be continually "filled with the Spirit." (Ephesians 5:18) Why did Paul tell them to be filled with Holy Spirit when they were already baptized with Him? The initial baptism in Holy Spirit does not mean we are going to automatically live a Spirit-filled life every minute. We are sinners who screw things up. Sometimes we fall off the wagon. At those times, we must repent and ask God to forgive us. He does and with our hearts clean again, Holy Spirit can lead us as He wills. This is the ongoing filling of Holy Spirit. (Ephesians 5:18)

I'm so glad God gave us this provision. We need to know we can return to Him when we sin. This is not an excuse to sin or make light of sin. Quite the opposite. Our heart's desire is best fulfilled when we obey Holy Spirit and live intimately with Him. Therefore, we repent and come back to Him after we have missed the mark.

One result of Holy Spirit filling us is that we become bold in our faith. Check out the story in which Peter and John were jailed for preaching Jesus. Peter was "filled with the Holy Spirit" when he addressed a Council who tried to curtail his efforts. (Acts 4:8) With his life on the line, he boldly preached the gospel to people who hated him. With Spirit-filled power, he stated this about Jesus: "There is salvation in no one else! God has given no other name under heaven by which we must be saved." (Acts 4:12) The Council afterward released Peter and John. They returned to their friends and reported what happened. Their friends became bold when they prayed, "And now, O Lord hear their threats, and give us, your servants great boldness in preaching your word. Stretch out your hand with healing power; may miraculous signs and wonders be done through the name of your holy servant Jesus." (Acts 4:29-30)

They did not feel sorry for themselves when someone rejected them. Instead they were filled with Holy Spirit, who seemed to say to them, *go big and go bold!* When they did, God answered their prayer. " . . . the meeting place shook, and they were all filled with the Holy Spirit. They preached the word of God with boldness." (Acts 4:31) They were ready to go out and be bold again. In essence, they said, "We don't care about ourselves as much as we care about obeying God and setting other people free in Jesus' name." They were similar to the believers in Revelation 12:11, "And they have defeated him by the blood of the Lamb and by their testimony. And they did not love their lives so much that they were afraid to die."

We see the boldness of Peter and other disciples when they were brought again to the same Council. They said, "We must obey God rather than any human authority . . . We are witnesses of these things and so is the Holy Spirit, who is given by God to those who obey him." (Acts 5:29-32) Note what Peter said in that last sentence about Holy Spirit, " . . . who is given by God to those who obey Him." It is from Him that we acquire our boldness.

Jesus, through Holy Spirit, was indeed busy in the lives of those earliest Christians who were His church. What He did through them He plans to do through us, the modern-day church.

CHAPTER 22

The King Creates His Church (33 AD)

"For the Son of Man came to seek and save those who are lost." (Luke 19:10)

THE WORLD IS GOING to hell. Who will help it avoid perdition?

God gave the answer when Jesus created the church. We will call the church the Body of Christ (also known as the Body of Believers). This body has become the offensive weapon against God's spiritual enemies under Holy Spirit's leadership. This group of New Testament people continued God's clarion call. They handed it on to the next generation, which passed it on to the next, and the next, until it has reached you and me. We continue the blitz and will hand it off to the next generation. This will continue until Jesus returns.

One of the greatest weapons against satan is the mind. Holy Spirit renews and enables the born-again mind to understand the main message in scripture—and to act on it. God uses our renewed minds as part of His plan to set the captives free. "Let this mind be in you which was also in Christ Jesus." **(Philippians 2:5 NKJV)** Think of it. God commands believers to have the same mind Jesus had! We must think and have the same attitudes He did.

Jesus' attitude toward unbelievers was that He loved them and wanted to redeem them for eternity. The church that teaches this same attitude is the Body of Christ. They understand Jesus came with agape love to set people free from their spiritual enemies.

Here is an example of how Jesus sets people free from the power of the devil. This is a phantasy type of story to get the point across.[21] Picture in your mind a raging, abusive dog owner. He is walking his ten dogs and controls them by the leash wrapped around his hand. As they walk, he curses and whips them. This happens every day. The dogs have never had another owner so they do not know what a kind owner would be like. They have grown accustomed to their tyrant so they take the ill treatment as best as they can.

Then one day they meet a kind stranger. He stops their owner and says to the dogs, "You don't have to take this torturous treatment. Follow me. I will set you free from your abusive owner. I will give you life that is full of meaning, along with what you need."

Five dogs accepted his offer. They were miraculously changed into new dogs. Their old, dead bodies laid on the ground next to them. Immediately their growling former owner curses them and begins to abuse them again.

The dogs cringe and take the abuse.

The new owner says to the five dogs, "Why are you still taking his abuse? You are now free to follow me. Come on!"

The dogs yelp, "We can't. We're tied to our master."

The new owner asked, "Where's your leash?"

They looked around. That is when they saw their leashes still around the necks of the dead bodies laying on the ground next to them. Then they realized they were free from their old master's control.

Often believers think or feel they are still under satan's control and act like it. Once we put our faith in Jesus, we need to thank Him for defeating our spiritual enemy—the devil and anything that still seems to influence us to sin. We need to step out in faith and celebrate the truth that sin no longer has power over us, but we have power over it. Sin lies powerless on the ground, like the leash still wrapped around the neck of our old, unbelieving nature.

In Christ, we are new creatures. We are no longer the unbelievers we used to be. In our new believing nature, we are no longer shackled to the devil and his evil. "Sin is no longer your master . . . Instead, you live under the freedom of God's grace." (Romans 6:14)

"My old self has been crucified with Christ. It is no longer I who live, but Christ lives in me. So, I live in this earthly body by trusting in the Son of God, who loved me and gave himself for me." (Galatians 2:20)

The church attacks and conquers evil by bringing the good news of salvation and freedom to our sick, pagan world. That Body of Christ blitzes the enemy as its Lord did when He was on this globe.

Some devil-captivated people come to believe the good news that the church tells them. God then uses the Body of Christ to rescue those new believers by releasing them from the devil's life-choking grip on their lives, as Jesus did. The church does this ministry in the name, authority, and power of Jesus, the Messiah. Through that ministry God restores people from captivity. He sets them free in areas like money, jobs, family, and from whatever hinders their walk.

Long before the church was even a concept in anyone's imagination, Jesus predicted that He would build His church. **(Matthew 16:13-18)** This is the first time in the Bible where the word *church* appears. Jesus brought this new mental image to His disciples well before He suffered and died. He was avant-garde. He was way ahead of His time with His unorthodox idea called, "the church."

He considered His new concept so important that He chose a most unlikely place to teach it to His followers. One day, He took His disciples on a thirty-two mile walk to a city called Caesarea Philippi. According to www.fishingtheabyss.com it was sin city—the "Las Vegas" of Jesus' time. Banias is its modern name, and the city is located near Mt. Hermon in the Golan Heights in northern Israel.

In Jesus' day, Caesarea Philippi was the religious center for the worship of the pagan fertility god, Pan, and other gods. It had a large cliff called Rock of the Gods. In front of that cliff, Pagans built religious shrines to various gods, including Caesar, Nemesis (the Roman god of justice), and Pan (which was surrounded by nymphs). Pan was pictured as half human and half goat. A grand cave stood in the center of the Rock of the Gods. It was called the Gates of Hell. People believed that the god Baal entered and left through that cave as he traveled to and from the netherworld. The Pan shrine was next to that cave and was the spot where pagans performed bizarre sexual rites.[22] This is the setting for Matthew 16:13-18.

Why did Jesus choose this place of filthiest morals to teach His disciples about His church? Within eyeshot, if not the actual location of the shrine, Jesus asked His disciples, " . . . who do you say that I am?"

Peter answered for the disciples when he said, "You are the Christ, the Son of the living God."

Jesus responded, "Blessed are you, Simon . . . for flesh and blood has not revealed this to you, but My Father who is in heaven . . . And I also say to you that you are Peter and on this rock, I will build My church, and the gates of Hades [Hell] shall not prevail against it." (Matthew 16:17-18 NKJV)

What was Jesus saying with His phrase "on this rock I will build my church?" The two traditional interpretations are, 1) since the name Peter meant *stone,* Jesus made a play on words that meant He would build His church on Peter as the rock; 2) others interpret that Jesus would build His church on Peter's *confession* that Jesus was the Christ. However, a third interpretation comes from the setting of the text. This interpretation teaches that Jesus meant the Rock of the Gods when He said, "on this rock I will build my church."

It was as if Jesus threw down the gauntlet to His enemies. He might have said, "As I stand on this rock I declare I will build my church. I am in your territory, lucifer, and I'm coming after you. The gates of hell will not be able to stop my church. My followers will break through your gates, enter your territory, and destroy you and your evil powers as they call people back to God from your evil clutches. Those who respond will enter the right relationship Adam and Eve had with God at Creation. Through my church I will give them eternal life."

The symbolism was rich. Jesus used real-world elements, such as the Rock of the Gods and the cave known as the Gates of Hell as symbols in the spiritual war He fought against the devil. That is where Jesus birthed His church.

He spoke to His disciples, who knew very well what the Rock of the Gods and the Gates of Hell were and what they stood for in pagan beliefs. Therefore, it would have been easy for them to understand that He used those props to make a spiritual point when He said, "on this rock" and "the gates of hell shall not prevail against it."

"It" refers to the church, the Body of Christ. Jesus pictures His church as an offensive weapon under the leadership of Holy Spirit. It is a battering ram, busting down the gates of hell, destroying the world's defenses, and invading the enemy's territory, just as her Commander-in-Chief had done earlier.

Hell's gates would not be able to stop the Body of Christ. The Gates of Hell defended, protected, and secured their fortress—hell. Gates are never offensive weapons. They are only defensive and gates are not able to prevail against the Body of Christ when she comes against them.

This was the vision Jesus had for His church. With this picture in His mind, He continued to wage war against the devil and his powers of hell. He would build His church on that vision. He saw her telling the truth: that He is the Messiah, the Son of the living God, who came to bring eternal freedom to our imprisoned world.

One might say, "God helps the world." Yet, He brings more than help. Through the Body of Christ, He brings healing, freedom, and eternity to a sick and dying world. As we saw in Matthew 16:13-18, Jesus planned all along to restore humans from captivity as He entered the devil's territory through His church.

But the Carpenter had to build His church before He could use it.

CHAPTER 23

The King Builds His Church (33 AD - Present)

"Together, we are his house, built on the foundation of the apostles, and the prophets. And the cornerstone is Christ Jesus himself." (Ephesians 2:20)

JESUS BUILT HIS TRUE church as an organism that has its own life. It is spiritual in nature. "For the kingdom of God is not a matter of eating and drinking, but of righteousness, peace and joy in the Holy Spirit." (Romans 14:17 NIV)

Righteousness means to be right with God, to live in right relationship with Him, and to do right things. *Peace* means to live in a peaceful relationship with God. Since we are united with God through Jesus our Mediator, there is no strife between Him and us. *Joy* refers to the gladness believers experience when God draws them back into that right relationship with Him. Romans 14:17 presents a picture of the type of people who are the true church. They believe in Jesus Christ as Savior and Lord, and experience the freedom He gave them.

They are the church—a living organism. One cannot build or shape an organism into a form with walls, a steeple, and a roof. The church organism is like an amoeba, a single-celled creature that has a jellylike body and is always moving. Therefore, it has no static shape. The true church of Jesus Christ has its own shape, which is spiritual, not physical. That organism derives its life from Holy Spirit and exists inside and outside the organized church.

There are true and false churches, but it is beyond the scope of this book to determine which churches are true or false. When I refer to the church, I mean the organism Paul described in Romans 14:17. With this in mind, I use the term "the church" with no other qualifications. God will judge whether churches are true or false.

After Jesus returned to heaven, He continued His onslaught on evil when He sent His Spirit to this world to take up residence in the hearts of believers. They follow Jesus and bring His help to our world through various ministries. These ministries are the same works Jesus did when He assaulted sin and evil by healing the sick, preaching the Kingdom of God, and setting the captives free.

Now watch the Carpenter build His church.

"So now you . . . are no longer strangers and foreigners. You are citizens along with all of God's holy people. You are members of God's family. Together, we are his house, built on the foundation of the apostles, and the prophets. And the cornerstone is Christ Jesus himself. We are carefully joined together in him becoming a holy temple for the Lord. Through him you . . . are also being made part of this dwelling where God lives by his Spirit." **(Ephesians 2:19-22)**

Jesus started a construction project when He became the Cornerstone for the foundation of His church. Next Jesus cemented in the disciples as the foundation to the building, along with the prophets. On that foundation, Jesus built the superstructure of the church. Symbolically, it included the floor, walls, ceiling, doors, windows, and roof. The symbolic superstructure represents believers who come to Jesus throughout history and become members of the Body of Christ.

At the point of faith, when people choose to believe in Jesus, Holy Spirit is in them and baptizes each new believer into the Body of Christ. "Some of us are Jews, some are Gentiles, some are slaves, and some are free. But we have all been baptized into one body by one Spirit, and we all share the same Spirit." **(1 Corinthians 12:13)** As Holy Spirit baptizes each believer into the Body of Christ, Jesus builds His church. We become the symbolic superstructure to the church.

Notice the method Jesus used when He built believers into His church. "And you are living stones that God is building into his spiritual temple." **(1 Peter 2:5)** The phrase "living stones" refers to believers.

Who builds them into the church?

Jesus does.

Observe the next phrase, "that God is building into His spiritual temple." God is the master mason who works through His Son as He picks up stones, rocks, or bricks, and trowels them with mortar, placing them into His superstructure called the church.

Does a brick do anything while the mason puts it into its place in the wall?

No, it is passive. The mason is active. A brick cannot build itself into a building.

You and I are bricks that Jesus cements into His Church.

The lesson we learn from this is that believers do not build God's church; God does. We are to submit ourselves to Jesus and let Him guide, direct, order, and place us as He sees fit. The more we move out of the way, the better Jesus can build His church.

There you have it! The Master Builder constructs the cornerstone, foundation, and structure into what is called the church, the Body of Christ.

God put the cornerstone in place when He sent Jesus to this world as its Messiah. He laid the foundation when He poured out His prophets and disciples as the concrete, upon which He planned to build His church. Now how does God build the structure?

The word *church* is derived from the Greek word, *ecclesia*, which literally means *God's called-out people*. When we come to believe in Jesus, God calls us out of this world's system of selfishness, rebellion, and sin into the right relationship with Him, in which we can freely love Him. This is the purpose for which He created humans in the first place.

People who are restored from captivity are those who live in a loving relationship with God and become more like Him. When this happens to us, we become the caring humans He wants us to be. We mirror Him as we continually agape love our neighbor. Where two or three or more of these agape-loving people gather together, there we make up the spiritual organism called the church that God uses to set pagans free from the devil. (Matthew 18:20)

We do not change the world by *going* to church; we change the world by *being* the church. The church is God's "called-out-ones," who destroy evil as they partner with God to set people free from the devil.

If the church does not do God's bidding, His will won't be accomplished. As Sabina Wurmbrand, co-founder of Voice of the Martyrs, said, "Doing the work of God is dangerous. Not doing it is more dangerous."[23] Who will bring freedom, healing, tell lost souls about Jesus, cast out demons, and work God's redemptive plan if not the church? The brave souls of His church do actions that accomplish God's mission.

If you are a true believer in Jesus, you are a part of God's Church, His Body of Believers, and called-out people. Together we are participants in His plan to restore humans from the grips of eternal captivity.

CHAPTER 24

The Church under the King's Authority (33 AD - Present)

"God has put all things under the authority of Christ and has made him head over . . . the church." (Ephesians 1:22)

GOD WORKED HIS TIME line for salvation through Jesus. He " . . . has now revealed to us his mysterious plan regarding Christ, a plan to fulfill his own good pleasure. *And this is the plan:* (emphasis mine) At the right time he will bring everything together under the authority of Christ—everything in heaven and on earth." (Ephesians 1:9, 10)

Jesus is the master mason who lays each brick and stone into its perfect spot. He does not ask our permission. He does as He pleases. He has total authority. God's plan to redeem His universe and people within it focuses entirely on Jesus, the authoritative Christ.

Think of it! Everything will come together under Christ's authority. What is everything?

It includes: the physical world, the unseen world, time, history, this life, and eternal life. The list is endless. God does not leave anything out. There is no one strong enough to be more authoritative than Jesus.

The Bible's central message of freedom is about Jesus coming to this world for everyone's good. No one can stop Jesus. The church is here to help fellow humans become free from hurt and wrong in areas such as broken relationships, injustice, or mental illness. This is the next stage in God's plan and explains why the church is not insignificant. In fact, God gave supernatural power to His Body of Believers.

> "I also pray that you will understand the incredible greatness of God's power for us who believe him. This is the same mighty power that raised Christ from the dead and seated him in the place of honor at God's right hand in the heavenly realms. Now he is far above any ruler or authority or power or leader or anything else – not only in this world but also in the world to come. God has put all things under the authority of Christ and has made him head over all things for the benefit of the church. And the church is his body; it is made full and complete by Christ, who fills all things everywhere with himself."
> **(Ephesians 1:19-23)**

We need to understand the incredible greatness of God's power for us who believe Him. The power that raised Jesus from the dead, which is the greatest strength on earth, is the same energy at work in the church. As Jesus was raised from the dead, so God raised followers of Christ from spiritual death when they believed in Jesus.

When Holy Spirit came, He brought Jesus' resurrection power and authority with Him. He is therefore able to do whatever He needs to through His Body of Believers. The church, therefore, is filled with Jesus Christ and His power because "God has put all things under the authority of Christ and has made him head over all things for the benefit of the church." (Ephesians 1:22)

Jesus is the most authoritative person in history. It is amazing enough that Jesus has authority over everything. It is downright dumbfounding to learn that His authority is "for the benefit of His church." (Ephesians 1:22) What does this mean?

The apostle Paul used the example of the human body when he called the church the Body of Christ. (Ephesians 1:23) The human body functions properly when all parts are in sync with each other. For example, our brain must be connected to our body in order to send signals through the nervous system. The Body of Christ has Jesus as its head. To function properly, the church must submit to Him to receive and carry out His directives.

God teaches us this profound truth: believers must understand that it's for *our* benefit that Jesus rules everything and everyone. Our leader, our Commander-in-Chief, is impervious and immune to, as well as inaccessible and unapproachable by, evil. The devil, his cohorts, nor anything evil can touch Him. That is why Jesus prefaced His Great Commission by saying, "I have been given all authority in heaven and on earth. Therefore, go . . ." (Matthew 28:18)

The church could not carry out her marching orders without Christ's leadership. Jesus, the authoritative One, provided that. In the early church, He raised up leaders, such as Peter, James, and John. He also called another man named Saul (later renamed Paul), to establish the Christian church worldwide among non-Jewish people. Up to that point in the central message, the earliest followers of Jesus were Jewish. God also wanted the rest of the world to believe in His Son, so He raised up Paul to bring the gospel to the non-Jewish (Gentile) world. It is likely most of us who read this book are non-Jewish. We can thank Paul for spreading the gospel in our direction. Here is the story of how the authoritative One brought Paul into leadership.

Paul, when he was first called Saul, was the leading enemy of the early Christian church. Jesus showed His authority and power over evil by performing a miracle on this murderous man when He caused a bright light from heaven to shine down on Saul and all around him.

Jesus literally knocked Saul off his horse while he was on his way to Damascus to imprison and kill Christians. **(Acts 9:1-20)** The Greek word for light is *phos*, from which we derive the word phosphorus. Phosphorus can cause an extremely bright and blinding light. I do not know how bright the light was that Jesus shined down on Saul, but he fell off his horse and was blinded. While lying on the ground he heard a voice; it was Jesus.

"Saul! Saul! Why are you persecuting me?"

"Who are you Lord?" Saul asked.

"I am Jesus, the one you are persecuting. Now get up and go into the city, and you will be told what you must do." (Acts 9:5, 6)

Do you see Jesus' authority and power here? This is not the sentimental, loving, tolerant, politically correct Jesus that so many believe in today. This is the Jesus who has authority over everything and everyone. This is the Son of God speaking from heaven to a murdering human, telling him what to do next. Jesus stopped this murderer in his tracks, and Saul immediately gave Jesus his undivided attention. Big, bad, boisterous, bragging, Saul was helpless and blind as his buddies led him to Damascus. He did not even eat or drink for three days, as he waited for further marching orders from his new Commander-in-Chief.

During those three days, Jesus appeared in a vision to another man named Ananias. He told Ananias to go to Saul, lay hands on him, and pray over him so he would regain his eyesight. He told Ananias, "Go, for Saul is my chosen instrument to take my message to the Gentiles and to kings as well as to the people of Israel." (Acts 9:15)

This is how Jesus chose Saul to be the lead man to bring the gospel to the world. It was no small feat. Saul, soon to be renamed Paul, led the charge to bring the gospel to Gentiles, the rest of the world, and ultimately, to us.

Paul became the most prolific writer of the New Testament. He wrote thirteen of its twenty-seven books. I like to refer to them as daggers. His books assaulted God's enemies as they brought the good news of Jesus to the world. These were letters to churches and individuals to whom he taught the truth about Jesus. God raised up many other leaders in His church, but through Paul and the disciples He provided needed leadership to His earliest church.

Jesus provided spiritual leadership to His church when He provided Holy Spirit on Pentecost. When Jesus provided leaders and Holy Spirit to His church, the church could then work in His authority. This means the church had power to use His name. For example, a policeman does not have physical power to stop an oncoming vehicle. However, all he has to do is raise his hand and the vehicle will stop. He stops that vehicle because he represents the power behind the law, and that forces the driver to stop. Likewise, we represent the one who has *all* authority. We fear no evil even when we suffer for our obedience, because we know we are under the authoritative One.

As British Prime Minister Winston Churchill discovered in World War II, blood, sweat, and tears were worth it. "Churchill himself framed the contest with Hitler as a 'battle for Christian civilization.' He insisted that 'Onward Christian Soldiers' be sung onboard the ship where he and Roosevelt forged their alliance against the Axis powers."[24]

We followers of Jesus will also have tough times in our war against evil. It doesn't have to be a war like WWII. It's a war in our lives on all levels. As with Winston Churchill, we follow our authoritative Leader.

CHAPTER 25

The King Equips His Church for Battle (33 AD - Present)

"A spiritual gift is given to each of us . . ." (1 Corinthians 12:7)

THE AUTHORITATIVE JESUS EQUIPPED His church so she could accomplish her mission. As the church goes worldwide to all nations, she will meet people of all types, races, and cultures. Along the way, she will also confront spiritual forces. The Bible calls these forces by many different names.

" . . . the *gods* in the heavens and the . . . *rulers* of the nations on earth." (Isaiah 24:21)

" . . . *authorities* in the unseen world." (Colossians 1:16)

" . . . the *devil* – the commander of the *powers* in the unseen world. He is the *spirit* at work in the hearts of those who refuse to obey God." (Ephesians 2:2)

" . . . *evil rulers*," "*authorities* of the unseen world," "*mighty powers* in this dark world" and "*evil spirits* in the heavenly places." (Ephesians 6:12)

" . . . *deceptive spirits* and teachings that come from *demons*." (1 Timothy 4:1)

It is impossible to categorize these forces into neat compartments. Sometimes, a spiritual force (let's call it sin), influences a person to do something wrong. For example, a teenager, with hormones raging, may give into the temptation to look at Internet porn. Sometimes a spirit being, such as a demon, might harass a human. For example, looking at porn may become a habit and the person gives him or herself over to it and loses control over the sin. That demon then has an opening in that life to harass the person continually. All spiritual forces influence humans.

For our purposes, let's categorize spiritual forces and spiritual beings as good or bad. Let's focus on angels. The good angels stayed loyal to God. The bad angels followed lucifer's lead and rebelled against God in heaven.

When God employs His church, He gives her marching orders to go on the offensive against the enemies of humanity, which includes angels who followed lucifer. " . . . we are not fighting against flesh-and-blood enemies, but against evil rulers and authorities of the unseen world, against mighty powers in this dark world, and against evil spirits in the heavenly places." (Ephesians 6:12)

The church's first line of spiritual battle is not against people, but against spiritual forces, those fallen angels that influence people. It stands to reason, therefore, that Jesus would not send His church to set people free from demonic influence without the ability to engage these spiritual forces. That is precisely why He equipped His church to meet them directly. This is war.

God succinctly stated His purpose for the church. "God's purpose . . . was to use the church to display his wisdom in its rich variety to all the unseen rulers and authorities in the heavenly places. This was his eternal plan, which he carried out through Christ Jesus our Lord." (Ephesians 3:10-11)

We are to display God's wisdom to all the unseen rulers and authorities in the heavenly places. We do not need to be afraid of them or ignore them. We must confront them and let God display His power through us.

The military commander equips his soldiers to defeat their enemies in war with proper leadership, military discipline, military doctrine (teaching), supplies, equipment, and armament. Similarly, Jesus equips His church to defeat her enemies in spiritual war with proper leadership, discipline, doctrine (teaching), supplies, equipment, and armament to defeat her enemies.

How did Jesus, our Commander-in-Chief, equip His spiritual army? First, He gave the church the best *leader* possible: Himself. "Christ is . . . the head of the church, which is his body." (Colossians 1:18) Our head, Christ, blitzed and defeated the devil and his evil forces during His life on earth.

The totality of God, including His power and authority, lived in Jesus' body. Now, Jesus lives in believers who are the Body of Christ. Think of it! The fullness of God, the Almighty Creator of the universe lives in the church. Here is the amazing scripture for this truth: "For in Christ lives all the fullness of God in a human body. So, you also are complete through your union with Christ, who is the head over every ruler and authority." (Colossians 2:9, 10)

Jesus wants to live His life through us. If we let Him, this is how He does it: His life is our source for everything. From *His* life, He gives *us* life. He gives us everything we need for this earthly life, such as His strength, His will, His power, His love, His grace, His mercy, His peace, His wisdom, His knowledge, and more. An intimate relationship with Jesus brings these attributes out in us when we submit to Him, follow His lead, and step out in faith. Jesus produces His life in us when we experience Him.[25]

Our Commander instills *discipline* into the members of His body. "But the Holy Spirit produces this kind of fruit in our lives . . . self-control." (Galatians 5:22-23) As we grow in our disciplined relationship with Jesus, Holy Spirit builds up the fruit of self-control in our character. We control ourselves to do what is right. Pleasing our Commander is the best form of discipline.

Our Lord gives *doctrine* (*teaching*) to His church. "For God loved the world so much that he gave his one and only Son, so that everyone who believes in him will not perish but have eternal life . . . There is no judgment against anyone who believes in him. But anyone who does not believe in him has already been judged for not believing in God's one and only Son." (John 3:16-18) This is at the core of the Bible's central message.

Our spiritual commander equips His church with *supplies* and *equipment*. We will focus on two categories: spiritual gifts and fruit.

Each believer has at least one spiritual gift. Holy Spirit gives them as He chooses. **(Ephesians 4:11-13, 1 Corinthians 12-14, Romans 12:6-8, and 1 Peter 4:10-11)** "It is the one and only Spirit who distributes all these gifts. He alone decides which gift each person should have." (1 Corinthians 12:11)

Here is a list of gifts with a definition for each: [26]
Administration: To steer the body toward the accomplishment of God-given goals and directives by planning, organizing, and supervising others. (1 Corinthians 12:28)

Apostle: To be sent to new frontiers with the gospel, providing leadership over church bodies with authority over spiritual matters. (Ephesians 4:11)

Celibacy: To voluntarily remain single without regret and with the ability to maintain controlled sexual impulses, to serve the Lord without distraction. (1 Corinthians 7:7, 8)

Discernment: To clearly distinguish truth from error by judging whether the behavior or teaching is from God, satan, human error, or human power. (1 Corinthians 12:10)

Evangelism: To be a messenger of the good news of the Gospel. (Ephesians 4:11)

Exhortation: To come alongside someone with words of encouragement, comfort, consolation, and counsel to help them be all God wants them to be. (Romans 12:8)

Faith: To be firmly persuaded of God's power and promises to accomplish His will and purpose. To display such a confidence in Him and His Word that circumstances and obstacles do not shake that conviction. (1 Corinthians 12:8-10)

Giving: To share what material resources you have with liberality and cheerfulness without thought of return. (Romans 12:8)

Healing: To be used as a means through which God makes people whole physically, emotionally, mentally, or spiritually. (1 Corinthians 12:9, 28, 30)

Help: To render support or assistance to others in the body to free them up for ministry. (1 Corinthians 12:28)

Hospitality: To warmly welcome people, even strangers, into one's home or church as a means of serving those in need of food or lodging. (1 Peter 4:9, 10)

Knowledge: To seek to learn as much about the Bible as possible through the gathering of much information and the analyzing of that data. [In addition, I would add: the ability to know something intuitively without having learned it in a traditional manner.] (1 Corinthians 12:8)

Leadership: To direct and motivate the church toward particular goals. (Romans 12:8)

Martyrdom: To give over one's life to suffer or to be put to death for the cause of Christ. (1 Corinthians 13:3)

Mercy: To be sensitive toward those who suffer . . . to feel genuine sympathy with their misery . . . [showing] compassion . . . deeds of love to alleviate distress. [Not to hurt or punish even when it is deserved.] (Romans 12:8)

Miracles: To be enabled by God to perform mighty deeds which witnesses acknowledge to be of supernatural origin and means. (1 Corinthians 12:10, 28)

Missionary: To be able to minister in another culture. (Ephesians 3:6-8)

Pastor: To be responsible to provide spiritual care, to protect, guide, teach, and feed spiritually a group of believers. (Ephesians 4:11)

Prophecy: To speak forth a prophetic message of God to His people. (Romans 12:6)

Service: To identify undone tasks in God's work, however menial, and use available resources to get the job done. (Romans 12:7)

Teaching: To instruct others in the Bible in a logical, systematic way to communicate pertinent information for true understanding and growth. (Romans 12:7)

Tongues: To speak in a language not previously learned so unbelievers can hear God's message in their own language for the body [of Christ] to be edified. (1 Corinthians 12:10; 14:27, 28)

Interpretations of Tongues: To translate the message of someone who has spoken in tongues. (1 Corinthians 12:10; 14:27, 28)

Voluntary Poverty: To purposely live an impoverished lifestyle to serve and aid others with your material resources. (1 Corinthians 13:3)

Wisdom: To apply knowledge to life in such a way as to make spiritual truths quite relevant and practical in proper decision-making and daily life situations. (1 Corinthians 12:8)

In addition to the gifts, Holy Spirit develops spiritual fruit in us.

Holy Spirit facilitates the growth of spiritual fruit in our lives as we mature in our experiences with Him. This fruit often grows best during difficult times. "But the Holy Spirit produces this kind of fruit in our lives: love, joy, peace, patience, kindness, goodness, faithfulness, gentleness, and self-control. There is no law against these things." **(Galatians 5:22-23)** Notice the Bible says, "There is no law against these things." In our freedom, Holy Spirit builds these traits into our character.

Lastly, God provides spiritual *armament* to His church. As a military commander provides weapons to his troops for battle, so God makes available spiritual armament to His troops for spiritual battle. ". . . put on every piece of God's armor so you will be able to resist the enemy in the time of evil . . . putting on the *belt of truth* and the body armor of *God's righteousness*. For shoes, put on the *peace* that comes from the Good News so that you will be fully prepared. In addition, . . . hold up the shield of *faith* to stop the fiery arrows of the devil. Put on *salvation* as your helmet, and take the *sword* of the Spirit, which is the word of God." [Emphasis mine] **(Ephesian 6:13-17)** In other words, be fully dressed and prepared for duty.

The list of armor consists of:
Truth: The truth that Jesus is the only way of salvation. "Jesus told him, 'I am the way, the truth, and the life. No one can come to the Father except through me.'" (John 14:6)
Righteousness: The follower of Christ is right with God. "For God made Christ . . . the offering for our sin, so that we could be made right with God through Christ." (2 Corinthians 5:21)
Gospel of Peace: Believers have peace with God. (Romans 5:1)
Shield of Faith: Faith is confidence and assurance. "Faith is the confidence that what we hope for will actually happen; it gives us assurance about things we cannot see." (Hebrews 11:1)
Salvation: Believers need to know they are saved. "I have written this to you who believe in the name of the Son of God, so that you may know you have eternal life." (1 John 5:13)
Sword of the Spirit: The Bible is our sword against our spiritual enemies. We need to follow Jesus' example when He answered the devil three times "it is written." (Luke 4:4,8,12 NKJV)

These pieces of armor are defensive in nature except the sword. They are defensive because the believer defends himself when the devil attacks with lies or deception. That is why the follower must be fully dressed and put on all the armor if he is to withstand his archenemy.

However, the pieces of armor become offensive weapons when the believer uses the Bible as his sword against the enemy. He does this by using biblical truth on any topic the devil is lying about. For example, after you commit a sin the devil may accuse you of being unredeemable and so bad that God has rejected you. You may feel like you have lost your salvation. However, your faith is based on what God says in the Bible, *not* on how you feel. With this knowledge, you can snap back at the enemy and say, "I know I sinned but I have repented, I feel remorse and changed my mind about my sin and have returned to God. Therefore, I am right with God." Luke 15:7 says, " . . . there is more joy in heaven over one lost sinner who repents and returns to God than over ninety-nine others who are righteous and haven't strayed away!"

Jesus equipped us with other offensive weapons:
Prayer: Prayer is communication with God. "Pray in the Spirit at all times and on every occasion. Stay alert and be persistent in your prayers . . ." (**Ephesians 6:18**)
Fasting: Fasting is not eating food, or abstaining from an activity for a period of time, while you prayerfully focus on God's help regarding an issue. " . . .when you fast, comb your hair and wash your face. Then no one will notice that you are fasting, except your Father who knows what you do in private. And your Father who sees everything will reward you." (**Matthew 6:17-18**)
Blood: When we "plead the blood" in prayer, we apply what Jesus accomplished on the cross to our situation. For example, an ex-convict in my Bible class felt that God had not fully forgiven him of his assault and battery charges. His fears were finally put to rest by this scripture: "All glory to him who loves us and has freed us from our sins by shedding his blood for us." (**Revelation 1:5**)

Jesus fills us with Himself, His life, spiritual gifts, spiritual fruit, armament, and weapons to fight our spiritual enemies. We use this equipment when we follow Jesus in our everyday lives and when we bring the good news of His freedom to the world. We are locked-and-loaded to "set the captives free." (Isaiah 61:1)

CHAPTER 26

Wasting Time with God
(33 AD - Present)

"For he . . . seated us with him in the heavenly realms . . ."
(Ephesians 2:6)

LIKE GOOD SOLDIERS, WE may have proper training and equipment, but how well do we know our commander? Military discipline teaches the soldier how to relate to his commander. The same is true for the spiritual military. The church needs to teach its members how to relate to their Commander—Jesus.

I am thankful for what I learned from my military commanders when I sat with them in Command and Control Centers. We can learn from our spiritual Commander, Jesus Christ, as we sit with Him, spiritually, in His Command and Control Room in heaven: "[God] . . . seated us with him in the heavenly realms." (Ephesians 2:6) Spiritually, we sit with the One who has all authority over our lives and the world. From this position, we learn what His perspective is toward our world. We then understand His nudges, prods, or still small voice, when He directs us to do something.

Dr. Henri Nouwen, a world-renowned priest and instructor at Notre Dame, Harvard, and Yale, taught me the life-changing truth of how to live in God's presence. He was a guest lecturer at the Air Force Chaplain School when I was on faculty. I had the duty and privilege of hosting Dr. Nouwen. In his lectures, he continually used the phrase "Wasting time with God." His point was that in our fast-moving society, we trick ourselves into thinking we are useful and valuable only when we are busy and active.

He offered our faculty and students an alternative. He suggested that we waste time with God. By "wasting," he meant we should spend time in God's presence by thinking about Him, focusing our minds on Him, praying to Him, reading His holy Word, and receiving His communication to us through His Word and answers to our prayers. To do this requires being focused on Him, quiet, still, listening to Him, and submitting in obedience. In the world's eyes, this probably looks like wasting time. In God's eyes, the most important thing a man or woman can do is to spend time alone with Him and learn from Him.

At the core, to waste time with God means to worship Him. Of course, worship can take multiple formats and includes public church services. However, here I emphasize worship as a lifestyle, a way of living in an intimate relationship with God. In that intimacy, we continually thank God for rescuing, freeing, and restoring us into right relationship with Him. This builds appreciation, respect, and trust into our relationship and results in our willingness to submit ourselves totally to Him. Then, as submitted believers, we yield to His will and know God better.

If God is truly God—the Supreme Being we worship—then we focus our attention on Him. He is the center of our world; we are not. We learn to wait on Him rather than come to Him with our list of things we want Him to bless or to do for us. He is not our spiritual Santa Claus, to whom we go with our wish list. Rather, He is the one and only true God to whom we owe all diligence. We bow down, worship, obey, and thank Him for the radical freedom He gave us. We do this because we owe Him everything, even our very life. This is wasting time with God.

Jesus is the Master Builder and He uses us as He builds His church. It is no longer about us " . . . getting a boost from Him, to do His work – but Him doing His work, and me borne along in His strength. The initiative, the idea, the direction, the empowering – and sustaining strength are all flowing from Him."[27] In His presence, I realize I cannot build His church, or His Kingdom for that matter, in my own strength. I just can't do it. "Then he spoke. At last you have seen it. You cannot do it. I have never asked you to do it. I, only I, can build my church. Will you stand aside, and let me build it through you?"[28]

Through wasting time with God, Jesus builds His church through submitted and disciplined followers. Let this be our response to Jesus: "Yes, Lord. Go ahead and do what you want. Apart from you, I can't do anything. The more I am patient in your presence and experience you in my life, the more I can do what you tell me to do and do it in your name, authority, and power."

As we waste time with God, He equips us the same way He equipped His earliest church. He gave Himself to them as their Leader. He gives Himself to us as our Leader. He produced His inspired, inerrant book, the Bible, to teach the early church correct doctrine. He offers the same to us. Twenty-one-hundred years ago, He equipped His spiritual militia with supernatural equipment and supplies, such as spiritual gifts and fruit. He equips us in the same way. He armed His earliest spiritual combatants with faith, prayer, and His blood to destroy the enemy of unbelief and build His Kingdom. He arms us identically. As football players go out of the locker room onto the field, equipped and ready, so we go out onto the field of life; we go equipped and ready to carry out our marching orders in our families, at our job, wherever we are.

Our Lord told us, " . . . anyone who believes in me will do the same works I have done, and even greater works, because I am going to be with the Father." (John 14:12) Apparently Jesus has confidence in His church. He said we would not only do the same works He did but we would do even greater works; greater in quantity around the globe, not quality. We could never improve on Jesus' quality of healing the sick or raising the dead.

Once Jesus reunited with His Father in heaven, He sent His Spirit to this world. Holy Spirit enters and lives in each believer around the globe. Believers waste time with Him; we sit with Him, learn from Him, and submit to Him. Through this action, Jesus instantly has global reach and worldwide power through Holy Spirit in His church. As we build His Kingdom in all countries, the gospel spreads over the entire earth. In this way, we do greater works. From heaven Jesus directs His spiritual militia in all countries simultaneously; billions of believers do His works all over the globe. The church is simultaneously a battleship fighting the enemy and a mercy ship bringing aid to the hurting human race by bringing them the gospel. She is not a cruise ship luxuriously enjoying herself.

Here is a historical snapshot of how Jesus launched His church:

- He first assigned marching orders to twelve disciples when He gave them authority to cast out evil spirits and to heal every kind of disease. (Matthew 10:1)

- Then, He sent out seventy-two others. (Luke 10:1-20) The church grew from twelve believers (Matthew 10:5) to eighty-four when Jesus added seventy-two others. (Luke 10:1)

- Minutes before He ascended back to heaven, Jesus sent His disciples out again, but this time to carry out The Great Commission, when He told them, "Go . . . in Jerusalem, Judea, Samaria, and to the ends of the earth." (Matthew 28:18-20 and Acts 1:8) They began in the city of Jerusalem, spread through the small country of Judea, expanded up north to the country of Samaria, and then to the rest of the world. (Matthew 28 and Acts 1)

- Before Pentecost, the eighty-four believers grew to 120. (Acts 1:15)
- On Pentecost, the number of believers explosively increased by around three thousand. (Acts 2:41)

This snapshot shows how the earliest church grew in numbers and geography within four years; from one man to multiple thousands.

The New Testament church implemented her marching orders magnificently. She is the perfect example of the Body of Christ wasting time with God. She received and obeyed her orders from Him. She defeated her enemies, brought God's good news to the world, rescued believers from their spiritual enemies, set people free in Jesus' name, restored them back to God, and built His Kingdom. Indeed, Jesus will say to her, " . . . Well done, my good and faithful servant." (Matthew 25:21)

Will He say that to us?

CHAPTER 27

Marching Orders
(33 AD – Present)

"And every day in the Temple and from house to house, they continued to teach and preach this message: 'Jesus is the Messiah.'" (Acts 5:42)

I REMEMBER THE OPENING night of the first Gulf War in Iraq, called Operation Desert Storm. It was January 1991. Our unit flew B-52 bombers. When our aircrews prepared for their first sorties over Iraq, headquarters ordered them to come in at low level as they approached their targets. That concerned us. Saddam Hussein was licking his chops, waiting for us with millions of rounds of anti-aircraft artillery (AAA). That was the firepower of choice to shoot down aircraft, especially the old, big, slow bombers we had.

Our unit had Pre-take-off Briefings (PTOBs) before every bombing run to prepare aircrews for their upcoming sorties. Among other things, the briefings included the air route the crews would fly, the type of weather they could expect, the altitude they should fly in, and duration of time for the sorties. A chaplain always ended the PTOB with prayer.

On this opening night of the war we feared we would lose a sizable percentage of our planes and crews to Saddam's AAA. We prayed hard.

After we completed the PTOB, I stationed my chaplain staff and myself at the doors to personally talk to each of the crew members as they filed out to the flight line to board their aircraft. One of the pilots handed me an envelope.

"What's this?" I asked.

"My wedding ring," he replied. "Please send it to my wife if I get shot down and don't make it back."

Chilling.

Not one plane was shot down.

That was military war. Our attention is on spiritual war. The above example of orders to send planes in at low level is similar to God ordering the church to go in at low level, house to house, and bring freedom to believers. "And every day in the Temple and from house to house, they continued to teach and preach this message: 'Jesus is the Messiah.'" (Acts 5:42)

Going house to house we engage personally with people of all types. Within our own families we mesh together. We help each other in our problems by applying what we know about God to that problem. At this level of engagement, we sometimes experience a hurt, confusion, a smiling face, or grin when a family member or friend listens to what we say.

The church is guaranteed to succeed due to Jesus' total authority and power. I will use the word WOE as an acrostic to explain this. The word woe usually means grief, regret, or distress. I do not use it in this context. Rather, the new association for woe makes it an exclamatory word when one speaks out suddenly in surprise, with passion. For example, when watching an Olympic runner break a world record you might say: "Did you see that burst of speed? He blew right by the other runners! Woe!"

The acrostic WOE is an example of Jesus' marching orders to the Body of Christ and exemplifies how God works through His church as an organism. The three letters represent three words: **W**orship, **O**bey, and **E**xplosion.

(**W**=*worship*): Believers live intimately with God.

(**O**=*obey*): Believers obey God when He gives a directive.

(**E**=*explosion*): After they obey, God brings an explosive impact.

Worship, as we have seen before, is more than worshipping God in a church service. For our purpose, we define worship as a lifestyle that brings glory to God as we live personally and intimately with Him. The believer who lives this life lives in peace and enjoys God's presence. That believer is ready to hear from the Lord and has a finely tuned, listening ear.

That believer is quick to obey whatever Holy Spirit directs.

The impact is explosive because it comes from God. His results may not always be explosive in our way of thinking, but often our Lord explodes onto the scene in ways to which we are not accustomed. Sometimes He works a miracle, wonder, or sign. At other times, His results are small or quiet, as with the "still small voice." (1 Kings 19:12 NIV) Quiet or mundane results are still explosive because they come from God and He makes the impact. Here are two scriptural examples of WOE:

1. While Moses stood on holy ground at the burning bush (W), God directed Moses to lead His people out of Egypt. During the Exodus God told Moses to raise his rod at the Red Sea. When he did (O) the waters parted (E). Moses didn't part the waters, God did. (Exodus chapters 3-14.)

2. In Athens Paul was troubled by all the idols he saw (W). He spoke to the city leaders about the idols and presented the Christian teaching about Jesus (O). Some of the city council members, Dionysius, Damaris, and others became believers (E). (Acts 17:16-34)

Notice that God, not people, initiated everything. The men were connected to God (W) so Holy Spirit could use them as He saw fit, anytime, anywhere. They did not dream up programs and then ask God to bless their efforts. They simply walked with the Lord and obeyed (O) Him as He led them to the next event in which He wanted to use them. After they obeyed, the Creator brought the result (E). Jesus said, "Come to me . . . My yoke is easy, my burden is light." (Matthew 11:28-30) We do not need to make ministry any harder than it is.

In these examples, none of the people performed miracles or converted anybody. God did. He changed hearts and worked the miracles. He still does today. As He used Moses and Paul, He wants to use us. Therefore, it is our privilege to obey our Commander-in-Chief as He gives us marching orders and we build His Kingdom. We need to leave the results up to Him.

The devil fears committed, obedient, prayerful believers because they tend to walk so close to God that they will obey Him no matter what. This gives God more opportunities to work His explosive impacts.

My college professor told our class one day, "Don't worry about your grades. Do your homework and the grades will be there." Spiritually, God says, "Don't worry about miracles. Simply walk with me (W), obey me (O), and the impact will be there (E)."

Believers are involved in spiritual warfare and the church is embroiled in it. We are at the epicenter of the war between God and the devil. As God works through us to accomplish His plans, He wants us to know that we must function totally within His power and authority. In this manner, He enables us to carry out His orders. With this knowledge and encouragement, we know we can.

He is the only God there is. Therefore, He is stronger than our enemies. Knowing that fact gives us confidence in the face of fear. That is why God says over three hundred times in the Bible, "Fear not."

Let's go into the world fully confident in our Commander. As we faithfully engage the broken world Jesus will display His power. That display is for the benefit of the church. It strengthens us in our faith and encourages us to continue to work with God and know Him better.

God gave His authority to His church when Jesus told His disciples, "Yes . . . I saw Satan fall from heaven like lightning! Look, I have given you authority over all the power of the enemy . . ." **(Luke 10:18-19)**

Think of it. We do not do God's work in our own puny, human strength. God dedicates Himself to His church as we obey Him. The church literally has God and His supernatural power and authority in her spiritual DNA. We, the church, assault God's enemies: evil spirits, evil governments, false religions, and false philosophies. We bring freedom to lost souls in God's name, power, and authority. That is one reason why believers must go into politics, government work, and the media. God brings His freedom to the masses through believers in these and other positions of influence.

God forges ahead with billions of followers. He destroys His spiritual enemies and builds His Kingdom by calling people out of the world to Himself. Then He sets them free from evil, sin, and guilt. The church, as His spiritual weapon, must always be on the offensive to bring this freedom to the masses. The Commander-in-Chief directs all who yield to Him, anywhere, anytime. The church is available to Him twenty-four hours a day, seven days a week, 365 days a year.

Jesus created and built His church, established Himself as her commander, equipped her for battle, spends time with His troops, and gives marching orders. We are ready for whatever He has planned for us.

CHAPTER 28

When Duty Calls (33 AD - Present)

"We . . . don't wage war as humans do . . ." (2 Corinthians 10:3-5)

JOSHUA AND THE NATION of Israel prepared to cross over the Jordan River. They were about to enter the promised land to live in freedom. (Joshua 3:1-16) Israel followed God (W) and He commanded the priests to step into the water. They obeyed (O), and the waters parted (E). The priests did not part the waters, God did . . . but not until the priests stepped into the water and wet their feet.

This is the paradigm for the church. We wage war, but not as humans normally do. We must wet our feet and part the spiritual waters so God can set people free from their spiritual enemies. Here are a few examples from the New Testament.

Holy Spirit prompted Peter to speak to a crippled man (W), Peter commanded the man to get up and walk (O), and God healed him (E). (Acts 3:4-8)

"We are human, but we don't wage war as humans do. We use God's mighty weapons, not worldly weapons, to knock down the strongholds of human reasoning and destroy false arguments. We destroy every proud obstacle that keeps people from knowing God. We capture their rebellious thoughts and teach them to obey Christ." **(2 Corinthians 10:3-5)** In this manner the church sets many people free.

Notice the spiritual warfare language. The purpose of the military is to keep peace and order, but sometimes it becomes necessary to break things and kill people to gain peace and order. The purpose of the militant church is to break things (such as spiritual strongholds and rebellious thoughts) and kill evil (such as false arguments and obstacles that keep people from knowing God). We do this by using our renewed minds and bringing good news to set our fellow humans free from evil's power.

The church has a double-edged sword in spiritual warfare: love and justice. The church teaches people about Christ (love) and attacks spiritual enemies such as evil thoughts and false teachings (justice). Some of the Corinthian believers walked in close relation with God (W), destroyed strongholds (O), and set people free (E).

The main character of the Bible, the Son of God (W) became a human being so He could die for us (O). Only in this way could He defeat the devil and set humans free from their fear of death (E). (Hebrews 2:14-15)

" . . . he has given us great and precious promises. These are the promises that enable you to share his divine nature and escape the world's corruption . . . the more you grow . . . the more productive and useful you will be in your knowledge of our Lord Jesus Christ." (2 Peter 1:4, 8) The truth that a human could share in God's divine nature blew people's minds; it probably still does today. Peter lived closely with God (W), taught this scripture (O), which resulted in people sharing God's divine nature (E).

"So, humble yourselves before God. Resist the devil, and he will flee from you . . . Humble yourselves before the Lord, and he will lift you up in honor." (James 4:7-10) The early church minced no words but spoke the truth in agape love. James was bold because he lived intimately with his Lord (W), he wrote the truth (O) so God would set believers free from the devil's tyranny and lift them up in honor (E).

" . . . pray in the power of the Holy Spirit . . . await the mercy of our Lord Jesus Christ who will bring you eternal life." (Jude 20-21) Jude walked close with his Lord (W), penned these verses (O), and God gave freedom (eternal life) to His people (E).

The early church understood her call to duty, stayed focused on Jesus, and brought His eternal freedom to whoever would receive it. The devil does not like Jesus or the church to invade his territory. Therefore, the church has a fight on her hands when she goes out to tell the world the good news about Jesus. That is one reason so many believers are afraid to share their faith in Christ. The early church did not shrink back from accomplishing her duty of speaking this truth. She followed Christ in her life (W) and taught scripture (O) so people could know God (E).

This sets the stage for our modern-day church. What will we do?

CHAPTER 29

It's Our Turn
(Present)

" . . . go, I am with you always even to the end of the age."
(Matthew 28:18-20)

WE HAVE STUDIED HOW the early church executed God's
plan. She focused on Jesus. He was God's way of bringing salvation and
freedom to humans. She accomplished her marching orders because
Jesus built, equipped, and cemented His relationship with her. After
twenty-one hundred years, it's our turn.

The New Testament church started in the gospels: Matthew, Mark,
Luke, and John. Then it exploded onto the scene in the book of Acts,
which is an historical book. We can continue to live that book as we
take our turn in God's plan. We can bring the good news of salvation to
our world. In so doing, we run alongside Peter, James, John, Paul, and
countless others. If we stay focused on Jesus as they did, we will teach
people the Bible's central message of freedom in Jesus. Our listeners will
understand the Bible and God better and be set free from sin and evil.
Then God will bring His explosive results into their lives. He has done
this for over two thousand years and is not about to quit now.

"Christ has no body now but yours.

No hands, no feet on earth but yours.

Yours are the eyes through which he looks compassion on this world.

Yours are the feet with which he walks to do good.

Yours are the hands through which he blesses all the world.

Yours are the hands, yours are the feet, yours are the eyes, you are His body.

Christ has no body now on earth but yours."

Teresa of Avila[29]

This is still true today. Holy Spirit baptized us into His body (the church). Therefore, we are Holy Spirit baptized human beings. That puts us under Jesus' authority. From our position of inferiority, we receive our marching orders from our Commander-in-Chief. When we witness about Jesus, we need to do it in the power of Holy Spirit and leave the results up to God our Father.

This kingdom pattern of evangelism is for all areas of life, wherever God works physically, mentally, emotionally, or spiritually. He will initiate the action and come to anyone whose heart is ripe for Him. Sometimes you will not know what He is up to, but that does not matter. Just obey and leave the results to Him.

One Sunday evening while I was preaching, God initiated an action. I heard a muffled scream about two-thirds back in the sanctuary. I saw several people quickly gather around a young lady. I paused as the congregation turned to tend to the commotion. In a few moments, one of the ushers told me that a woman had been healed of a goiter. One moment it was there, the next, it was gone. She felt the healing and screamed. As she told her friends sitting next to her what had happened, others also noticed the goiter had disappeared. It was a vintage expression from God. He told the church to worship (W), we obeyed (O), and He healed (E). He will not always use miracles, although they should be a part of our normal Christian life.

Do you ever wonder what it means to be led by Holy Spirit? As we live in an intimate relationship with Him, He initiates the action: a thought, a nudge, an impression, idea, event, circumstance, prayer, reading, or whatever He wants to use to prompt us to obey Him. Sometimes, His attention-getting devices are loud; other times a whisper. If we are living intimately with Him, He will teach us His ways and we will learn to recognize when He calls us to action. We are caught up into the very plan God started in the Garden of Eden, continued through the Old and New Testaments, and carried through two thousand one hundred years of history. Now He rolls into our era. Holy Spirit sweeps us up and carries us along for the ride because He plans to use us in His work.

Enter the modern church. By modern church I mean the Body of Christ in our day, that organism of true believers around the world. The most recent church on the scene—us. I do not mean the modernistic church that adopts and adapts to modern theologies and religions that seemingly accepts and tolerates all pluralistic and diverse methods of salvation.

For the modern church to fully participate with God to carry out His plan, we are duty-bound to heed Paul's advice to us. "Soldiers don't get tied up in the affairs of civilian life, for then they cannot please the officer who enlisted them." (2 Timothy 2:3-4) God is the officer who enlisted us through Holy Spirit's nudges. We are to stay focused on Him, not become tied up in affairs of the world.

When I served in the U.S. military I learned why it is necessary to obey my commanders. The military could not function if soldiers, airmen, sailors, marines, or coastguardsmen did not obey their commanders. That is also true for God's spiritual military. We are His battleship fighting sin, lies, temptations, drugs, deceit, and lust. Freedom from these things hangs in the balance and our obedience as a mercy ship opens the door for Holy Spirit to do His work through us to set people free.

Jesus told the church, "To all who are victorious, who obey me to the very end, to them I will give authority over all the nations . . . They will have the same authority I received from my Father." (Revelation 2:26-28)

Did you catch that? Jesus will give His authority to believers who are victorious, to those who obey Him to the end. That includes us.

One of the ways Jesus passed on His authority to His disciples was to teach them how to pray. After His disciples asked Him to teach them to pray, He responded. "When you pray, say: 'Father, hallowed be your name, your kingdom come. Give us each day our daily bread. Forgive us our sins, for we also forgive everyone who sins against us. And lead us not into temptation.'" (Luke 11:1-4 NIV)

Jesus began His teaching on prayer with a command when He introduced the Lord's Prayer with a one-word order: "say." The verb "say" is in the imperative mood, which means to speak as a command or authoritatively. He commanded His disciples to pray with authority as He did.

The first four verbs in the Lord's Prayer are "hallowed," "come," "give," and "forgive." Each is in the imperative mood. It's as if Jesus said to His followers, "You asked me to teach you how to pray. Okay, I will. I pray with authority so I often use commands because it is imperative that I pray what my Father wants me to pray for. You do the same. I'm giving you authority to pray as I do."

Many modern church members do not realize that the Lord's Prayer is a prayer of command. We must pray with imperative urgency, not by mesmerized, monotonous, memory. Jesus' one-word command "say" takes the Lord's Prayer out of the realm of mindless repetition and elevates it into the realm of authority.

That does not mean we are to always command something in prayer. Rather, it means we pray authoritatively because what our Father directs us to pray for is important. Therefore, we emphatically pray, "hallowed be Thy name," "Thy kingdom come," "Thy will be done," "forgive us our sins." Then, we teach others to pray this way.

We have seen runners hand off batons to other runners in relay races. As if she were in a relay race, the New Testament church handed off its baton of authority to the first-century church, who handed it off to the next generation, who handed it off to the next, and the next, down through the ages, all the way to our generation. Envision the church from the last generation . . . she's running up behind us with the baton in her hand. As she stretches out her hand to put the baton into our hand, we start our run and put our hand out behind us to receive that baton. Once we feel the baton slapped into our hand, we kick ourselves into high gear to carry our authority as we run the race ahead of us, blitzing the enemy and setting people free as we go.

A defensive army has never won a war and this is true in spiritual warfare also. Remember, Jesus said the gates of hell would not prevail against His church. The gates of hell symbolize satan's grip on people. The church is the battering ram that loosens satan's grip on humanity. When we bring the gospel, God releases believers from their prison of sin and evil.

That offensive church gains spiritual victories while she is on the march. She has the initiative to bring the gospel to others and set them free from evil. We do not have to *be* offensive; we have to be *on* the offensive. We go; we do not stand still. We make disciples; they do not come out of thin air. We baptize them, thereby telling the world "this baptized person belongs to Jesus." We teach disciples to obey Jesus. Obedience is not learned overnight.

We do this with explosive impact because Jesus, our Commander-in-Chief, explodes His acceptance, forgiveness, grace, love, and justice into believers' hearts when the enemies of doubt, fear, and cynicism are destroyed. This is our global ministry. From America to China, from

Korea to Saudi Arabia, country to country, and continent to continent. Believers waste time with God (W), follow Holy Spirit's nudges by doing what He tells us to do (O), then it is up to God to work His explosive results (E).

The story of the valley of dry bones in Ezekiel 37:1-14 crystallizes the truth for how God brings freedom and life. God took hold of the prophet Ezekiel. When God takes hold of you, you are in a very tight relationship! God showed Ezekiel a valley filled with dry bones and told him to speak the following prophetic message to them, "Dry bones, listen to the word of the Lord! This is what the Sovereign Lord says: 'Look! I am going to put breath into you and make you live again! I will put flesh and muscles on you and cover you with skin. I will put breath into you, and you will come to life. Then you will know that I am the Lord.'" (Ezekiel 37:1-6)

Ezekiel obeyed (O). "So, I spoke this message, just as he told me." (Ezekiel 37:7)

"Suddenly, as I spoke, there was a rattling noise across the valley. The bones of each body came together and attached themselves as complete skeletons. Then as I watched, muscles and flesh formed over the bones. Then skin formed to cover their bodies but they still had no breath in them." (Verses 7-8)

"Then he said to me, 'Speak a prophetic message to the winds, son of man . . . and say, this is what the Sovereign Lord says: Come, O breath, from the four winds! Breathe into these dead bodies so they may live again'" (Verse 9)

"So, I spoke the message as he commanded me . . ." (Ezekiel 37:10)

" . . . and breath came into their bodies. They all came to life and stood up on their feet—a great army." (Verse 10)

The valley of dry bones is a metaphor. Ezekiel faced an impossible task because he could not give life to old, dry bones that represented the unbelieving Israelites in his day. Yet, he did what God told him to do and God brought His explosive result of life to those dead bones.

We modern believers face a country and world in which we see overwhelming spiritual death, like the dry bones in the book of Ezekiel. It is not up to us to bring life into those bones. That is God's job. Our job is simply to speak to them what God tells us to say. If we obey like Ezekiel did, God will bring His life into the lives to whom we speak.

By His "life" I mean the essence of life only God possesses: uncreated, eternal life. Humans do not have that life. We have only biological and psychological life. God shares His eternal life with those who believe in Jesus as their Savior and Lord. By that life God sets people free from their prisons. He restores us from temptations we give in to, from inner desires that are wrong, from lack of self-control, from broken relationships, from always being in need, and a host of other issues. It is our turn to bring this good news to hurting people.

CHAPTER 30

Where's the Stuff?
(Present)

"And now O Lord . . . give us . . . great boldness. Stretch out your hand with healing power; may miraculous signs and wonders, be done through the name of your holy servant Jesus." (Acts 4:29, 30)

WHEREVER JESUS WENT, HE worked miracles. It was natural for Him. His earliest church followed in His footprints and continued His explosions, which were also natural for the church. Why? Just as Jesus was intimate with His Father, the church was intimate with Jesus. In return, He could naturally work His miracles through His Body of Believers. He continued this method of operation throughout history, right down to our time.

So, "where's the stuff?"

A new believer asked that question soon after Jesus set him free from sin. At one point, while his pastors took him through the books of Matthew, Mark, Luke, John, and Acts to show him the mighty works of Jesus and the early church, he blurted out in confused enthusiasm, "Where's the stuff?!"

"What stuff?" the pastors asked.

"The signs, wonders, and miracles you told me about," he replied.

He did not see those powerful works in his church, so in his youthful innocence, naiveté, and exuberance, he gushed the question, "Where's the stuff?"

It's a great question; a legitimate one that deserves an answer.

"Stuff," like signs, wonders, and miracles do not always happen. However, we should see them as visible affirmations of God's love and power when they do happen. Jesus' disciples returned and reported to Him that demons obeyed them when they used His name. That happened after He sent them out under His authority. They had no seminary or Bible school diploma, yet lots of "stuff" validated their ministry. Nevertheless, Jesus told them, " . . . don't rejoice because evil spirits obey you; rejoice because your names are registered in heaven." (Luke 10:20)

First, it is most important to know that we have salvation, freedom, and eternity with our Lord in heaven. Salvation and freedom from sin are already "stuff." In fact, they are the most important "stuff" that count for eternity.

Other "stuff," like miracles, should be normal in everything the church does, just as in the days of Jesus and the earliest church. Jesus never said miracles would stop someday or just fade away. Evidently, the earliest church continued them. Luke recorded miracles in the book of Acts and the church has perpetuated them throughout history. In the historical sense, there is no end to the book of Acts. The church has not finished her work yet. Jesus will continue to work His "stuff" through His Spirit-filled church until He returns.

Here are a few historical events in which God showed His "stuff":

The Reformation started in the sixteenth century. Through reformers such as John Huss (who was burned at the stake), John Wycliffe, and others, God ushered in the Protestant Reformation, with its emphasis on the Bible. The Reformation contained a lot of Holy Spirit "stuff." Men like Martin Luther, John Calvin, John Knox, and others emphasized the central message that Jesus brought redemption to this earth. This caused the Reformation to spread throughout Europe like wildfire.

The Reformation laid the foundation for the gospel to spread to the United States and other countries around the world. Not all nations were converted, but the gospel went global and continues to do so today. The agape love of God spread, not only by evangelism, but also through the building of hospitals and bringing of medical aid to countries in desperate need. Christian ethics were instilled into politics and social life as never before.

In the seventeenth century, Pilgrims and Puritans, along with many other believers, brought the gospel to the United Sates. Many Christians were leaders in the formation of our country. They instilled their teachings, ethics, beliefs, and practices into our political system. Two of the highlights of their work are the Constitution of the United States and the Declaration of Independence.

In the eighteenth and nineteenth centuries, evangelists spread the gospel throughout the United States. Many new Protestant denominations, such as Methodist and Baptist, were established. That resulted in many areas of America becoming saturated with Christian churches. The best known might be a large portion of the southern United States, called the Bible belt.

In the early twentieth century, Holy Spirit broke out in Pasadena, California at the Azusa Street Revival. That revival birthed the worldwide Pentecostal movement that continues around the globe in our time.

In our twenty-first century, Holy Spirit is leading His church in new and dynamic ways outside the United States. For example, God is raising up the Episcopal church in Africa; Holy Spirit is sparking spiritual movements in South America, Korea, and China; and even inside Islam many are coming to faith in Jesus Christ throughout the Middle East and Asia.

In the twenty-first century, we see much of the leadership in the Christian church has moved from Europe and the United States to Africa, South America, and Asia, with over two billion believers in Jesus Christ worldwide.[30] Truly our Creator God is busy at work in the backyards of all the world's interconnected nations, spreading the Bible's central message of freedom in Jesus the Messiah.

K.P. Yohanan, founder of Gospel for Asia, put it this way:

> When we go to the book of Acts, we find the disciples totally convinced about the lostness of man without Christ. Not even persecution could stop them from calling people everywhere to repent and turn to Christ.
>
> Paul cries out in Romans 10:9-15 for the urgency of preaching Christ. In his day, the social and economic problems . . . were the same or worse than we face today. Yet the apostles did not set out to establish social relief centers, hospitals or educational institutions. Paul declared in 1 Corinthians 2:1-2, "When I came to you, . . . I determined not to know anything among you, save Jesus Christ, and him crucified." Paul recognized that Jesus Christ was the ultimate answer . . . you cannot miss the primary emphasis of his life and message.[31]

The history we just referred to is in some sense, a result of the Reformation; the Bible was distributed into people's hands around the world. They could read it for themselves and know God. They learned the central message that Jesus came to this world to set humanity free from the devil.

If we look at our marching orders, we see that Jesus has not rescinded one word from His Great Commission twenty-one centuries ago. His authority is global. God is showing His "stuff" around the world.

I was in a Middle Eastern country where I learned about an underground Christian church with believers who had converted from Islam to Christianity. The stress and dangers these Christians lived under were unbelievable. Families completely rejected or killed any family member who believed in Jesus. Knowing they could be caught, those believers did not shrink back, but focused on Jesus and committed their lives to Him. They had a comfort inside of them that strengthened them against persecution. The Heidelberg Catechism says in its first question and answer:

Q. "What is your only comfort in life and in death?"

A. "That I am not my own, but belong – body and soul, in life and in death – to my faithful Savior Jesus Christ."[32] Those converted Muslims experienced that comfort. This is Holy Spirit "stuff."

Another example of Jesus showing His "stuff" to Muslims comes from one of the best books I've read on Islam: *A Wind in the House of Islam* by David Garrison. He teaches that after the Prophet Mohammad started the Islamic religion in the seventh century there were no recorded converts from Islam to Christianity until the eighteenth century. Eleven centuries is a long time with no converts. In the nineteenth century over a thousand baptisms were recorded. The twentieth century showed a significant increase, to approximately eleven thousand baptisms, or eleven hundred new Christian churches within Islamic nations. Now for the explosion: in the first twelve years of the twenty-first century there are approximately sixty-nine thousand baptisms or sixty-nine hundred church starts in Muslim countries.[33]

God is using three effective tools to proclaim the message of Jesus to Islamic nations: visions, dreams, and the *Jesus* film. Reports come to Christian missionaries, evangelists, pastors, and others as they connect with these converts. Seeing Jesus in a vision or dream plants the seed for faith, and faith is sprouting throughout the Islamic world. God is also using the *Jesus* film, produced by Campus Crusade (www.cru.

org). By God's innovation, these three methods have reached unknown numbers of believers in Islamic nations around our globe. Through His twenty-first century church, God continues His signs, wonders, and miracles, His "stuff."

Today's modern church has the privilege of continuing the book of Acts by following Holy Spirit into Islam, and all parts of our world, to bring Muslims, Hindus, Buddhists, and others into God's Kingdom. There are millions of Chinese and Indians coming to faith in Christ, and there is a Third Wave of Holy Spirit in South America and Africa.

We live in a dramatic time in the Bible's central message. The global momentum is building as the velocity of setting people free from evil increases. We are blessed to be a part of that. "Where's the stuff?" It is all over the world. If believers live intimately with God, learn His will for freedom, and pray authoritatively, we will carry Jesus' baton of authority and continue to set people free from the devil and sin.

Could we be the people to usher in the end time when Jesus checkmates His enemy?

CHAPTER 31

Checkmate
(Date = the end of time)

"Then the devil . . . was thrown into the . . . lake of burning sulfur . . ." (Revelation 20:10)

CHESS PLAYERS END THEIR game when one maneuvers the opponent's king into a position from which he cannot escape. Checkmate. In tracing the Bible's central message of Jesus bringing freedom, we approach the end of the celestial chess match between God and lucifer. Jesus is about to return to this earth to checkmate His opponent.

When Jesus returns, God will actuate some mind-numbing, earth-shattering events to end this spiritual war. Jesus will set believers free from their graves, and believers still living on earth will be taken with them from this world. All believers will meet their Lord in the air and be taken up into heaven. This is commonly called the rapture.

"For the Lord, himself will come down from heaven with a commanding shout, with the voice of the archangel and with the trumpet call of God. First the Christians who have died will rise from their graves. Then, together with them, we who are still alive and remain on the earth will be caught up in the clouds to meet the Lord in the air. Then we will be with the Lord forever. So, encourage each other with these words." **(1 Thessalonians 4:16-18)**

Jesus is so trustworthy. Before His death, He promised His disciples, "Remember what I told you: I am going away, but I will come back to you again." (John 14:28) He came back when He rose from the dead and will come again at His second coming.

At His return, believers around the globe will rise from their graves. "But there is an order to this resurrection: Christ was raised as the first of the harvest; then all who belong to Christ will be raised when he comes back." (1 Corinthians 15:23)

God raised Jesus from the dead Easter Sunday morning. All people throughout history who responded to Jesus' call to freedom will be raised from the dead. All believers who are alive when He returns will be caught up in the clouds to meet the Lord in the air with the resurrected believers. Per our Lord's consistent efficiency, He initiates everything. We don't. Somehow, in His power we will rise into the air to be with Him forever. Wow!

"So, encourage each other with these words." (1 Thessalonians 4:18) We encourage others and receive encouragement when we look expectantly toward Jesus' second coming. It will be glorious, exciting, and exhilarating to rise into the air and be with our Master for eternity. Welcome home, child of God, eternity has arrived. No wonder we look forward to His coming.

"After that the end will come." (1 Corinthians 15:24) The two words "after that" imply a period of time after the believers were raised from the dead but before the end comes. That is the space in which some huge events occur. It is what we call the end times.

There are three general views about how the end times will occur.

1. Pre-millennialism: This theory teaches that Jesus will return to earth before His one-thousand-year reign. This belief has various forms,

one of which includes time-based (dispensational) teachings about pre-tribulation rapture, mid-tribulation rapture, or post-tribulation rapture.

2. A-millennialism: This theory believes that the one-thousand-year reign is symbolic.

3. Post-millennialism: This theory teaches that Jesus will return after a one-thousand-year period of peace on earth.

I'm a "pan-millennialist," meaning that everything will "pan out" in the end. My purpose in this book is to trace the central message in the Bible as best as we can from beginning to end. We want to do that without becoming bogged down in any specific theory of the end times. Only God knows how or when the second coming will occur. The meanings of the end time events speak for themselves. By faith, we must learn what God teaches in them.

After the dead are raised and the rapture has occurred, the next earth-shattering event will take place when Jesus destroys His enemies. God promised in the Garden of Eden that He would send someone to crush the head of the snake. He is about to deliver on that promise. **(Revelation 19:11-21** and **Revelation 20:7-10)** The book of Revelation describes the Battle of Armageddon, the bloodiest battle this world will ever experience. In it, Jesus destroys His enemies as listed below.

Unbelievers – Those who do not believe in Jesus as their Messiah.

"There is no judgment against anyone who believes in him. But anyone who does not believe in him has already been judged for not believing in God's one and only Son." (John 3:18)

"And anyone whose name was not found recorded in the Book of Life was thrown into the lake of fire." (Revelation 20:15)

Babylon – Babylon is not only the city of Babylon. Babylon also refers to any spirit that vaunts itself against God, such as sensuous living, immorality, lust, pride, arrogance, greed, selfishness, a haughty attitude, and so on.

> " . . . Babylon is fallen . . . She will be completely consumed by fire, for the Lord God who judges her is mighty." (Revelation 18:2, 8)

The Beast – The beast represents a spirit, fallen angel, or demon that caused governments to rebel against God. God will destroy this evil spirit, along with the governments that followed it.

> "Then I saw the beast and the kings of the world and their armies gathered together to fight against the one sitting on the horse and his army. And the beast was captured . . . thrown alive into the fiery lake of burning sulfur." (Revelation 19:19, 20)

The False Prophet – The false prophet is a spirit that spawned false teachings, philosophies, and religions that rebelled against God.

> "And the . . . false prophet who did mighty miracles on behalf of the beast – miracles that deceived all who had accepted the mark of the beast and who worshiped his statue . . . [was] thrown alive into the fiery lake of burning sulfur." (Revelation 19:20)

The Devil – The devil refers to lucifer who deceived Adam and Eve so they would rebel against God in the Garden of Eden.

> "Then the devil, who had deceived them, was thrown into the fiery lake of burning sulfur, joining the beast and the false prophet . . ." (Revelation 20:10)

God prophesied the justice component in His freedom plan way back when He said, " . . . he will crush your head . . ." (Genesis 3:15 NIV)

That refers to Jesus destroying the devil. God will fulfill that prophecy when He throws the devil into the burning lake of fire, called Gehenna. (Revelation 20:10)

Checkmate.

"After that the end will come when he will turn the Kingdom over to God the Father, having destroyed every ruler and authority and power. For Christ must reign until he humbles all his enemies beneath his feet." (1 Corinthians 15:24-25)

The next mind-numbing event will be the great judgment. John described the scene. He saw God sitting on the great white throne. When He appeared, earth and sky fled from his presence. Then all the dead people from all history stood in front of Him. **(Revelation 20:11-15)** Imagine billions of people brought back to life.

In John's vision, all of them stood in front of the great judge while books were opened, including the Book of Life. Everyone was judged according to what they had done. Anyone whose name was not found in the Book of Life was thrown into the lake of fire.

That lake is not God's will for people, but the just and righteous judge who created the universe will use it if He must. Therefore, the church needs to ask unbelievers, "Why do you want to fight against God when He will judge you in the end?" That's precisely why Jesus gave this foreboding teaching: "But I'll tell you who to fear. Fear God who has the power to kill you and then throw you into hell. Yes, he's the one to fear." (Luke 12:5)

After the judgment, death and the grave were thrown into the lake of fire to join God's five other enemies. Add these two to the first five, and we have seven enemies that God totally destroyed:

1. Unbelievers
2. Babylon
3. The beast

4. The false prophet

5. The devil

6. Death

7. The grave.

Seven is the number of completion.[34] In John's vision, God obliterated His enemies once and for all. Checkmate.

CHAPTER 32

Mission Complete
(Future date = just before
eternity begins)

"After that the end will come, when he [Jesus] will turn the Kingdom over to God the Father . . ." (1 Corinthians 15:24)

SEVEN IS THE NUMBER for completion but also perfection and heaven. At this point in the central story, Jesus completed His assigned task with perfection. He destroyed His enemies and brought freedom to His people. He restored His believers into perfect relationship with God in heaven for eternity. Upon that perfect completion, He will perform the greatest hand-off in history when He turns the Kingdom over to His Father. " . . . then, when all things are under his [Father's] authority, the Son will put himself under God's authority, so that God, who gave his Son authority over all things, will be utterly supreme over everything everywhere." **(1 Corinthians 15:24, 28)**

Upon completion of that transaction, God will bring His plan to a perfect closure. He will create a new heaven and a new earth as the residence for humanity, that perfect place for believers in Christ to live with God in eternity. "No eye has seen, no ear has heard, and no mind has imagined what God has prepared for those who love him." (1 Corinthians 2:9)

"Then I saw a new heaven and a new earth, for the old heaven and the old earth had disappeared . . . I saw the holy city . . . coming down from God out of heaven . . . God's home is now among his people . . . He will wipe every tear from their eyes, and there will be no more death or sorrow or crying or pain. All these things are gone forever . . . All who are victorious will inherit all these blessings." **(Revelation 21:1-7)** All the blood, sweat, and tears of billions of believers will be worth it as they inherit their eternal home.

After God creates the new heavens and earth, He will say, "It is finished. I am the Alpha and the Omega, the Beginning and the End. To all who are thirsty I will give freely from the springs of the water of life." **(Revelation 21:6)**

Followers of Christ are in a win-win position. When we become children of the Lord, we win because Jesus immediately gives us supernatural freedom and eternal life at that moment and for our lives while we are still on earth. Through that freedom and life, we come to know God. When we die, we also win because we go immediately to be with our Lord in eternity. As the apostle Paul said: "For to me, living means living for Christ, and dying is even better." (Philippians 1:21) If Jesus returns before we die, believers win because He raptures us out of this world and takes us to heaven with Him. If we die before He returns, we win because He raises us from the dead and takes us to heaven. It does not matter when we live or die, we will be with our Lord.

Jesus reminds us one last time that He is the Root of David and heir to his throne. **(Revelation 22:16)** "Root" means He is the source from whom David came. "Heir" means He is the promised Messiah who would inherit David's throne and rule from it forever. By this statement Jesus confirmed that the Bible's central message is about Him, and confirms that God carried out His freedom plan through Jesus.

We traced the Bible's central message of freedom from beginning to end, Genesis through Revelation. At the finish line God said, "It is finished."

Mission complete.

CHAPTER 33

You Can Take It with You (Eternity)

"After this I saw a vast crowd . . ." (Revelation 7:9)

GOD DID IT. HE delivered on His promise (Genesis 3:15) to destroy His enemy and set His people free.

We traced the central message from start to finish; Eden to eternity. We even discovered where we fit into that plan. At the end of the story, believers find ourselves free and in heaven.

You've probably heard the statement: "You can't take it with you." I beg to differ. You can take it with you. Our riches transfer easily and perfectly into heaven. Our riches include: freedom, repentance, forgiveness, salvation, righteousness, obedience, love, self-control and a host of others. God gave us freedom right here on earth, and we take that to heaven with us.

What will heaven be like?

" . . . I saw a vast crowd, too great to count, from every nation and tribe and people and language, standing in front of the throne and before the Lamb. They were clothed in white robes and held palm branches in their hands. And they were shouting with a great roar, 'Salvation

comes from our God who sits on the throne and from the Lamb!'"
(Revelation 7:9-10)

We will be so overjoyed, overcome, and overwhelmed that we won't be able to help or contain ourselves. We will break out in perfect praise to God for His gift of eternal freedom. We will rejoice by choice. Just think of it; we will live in a perfect place, in impeccable conditions, a flawless life that never ends. It does not get any better than that.

God's people will be too many to count. Does this remind you of anything? God set up His plan when He told Abraham: "Look up into the sky and count the stars if you can. That's how many descendants you will have!" (Genesis 15:5) Abraham believed God, and He counted him as righteous because of his faith. This promise is fulfilled in Revelation 7:9-10.

Believers from all seven continents will be included in Abraham's descendants: Africans, Asians, Australians, Europeans, North Americans, South Americans, and even Antarcticans (if there were any)! All types and colors of people will be in heaven. As the children's song goes, "Red, brown, yellow, black, and white, they are all precious in His sight."[35]

This fulfills God's prophecy to Abraham: "I will certainly bless you. I will multiply your descendants beyond number, like the stars in the sky and the sands on the seashore . . . And through your descendants all the nations of the earth will be blessed – all because you have obeyed me." (Genesis 22:17-18) This fulfillment proves humans can trust God to keep His promises to Abraham (around 2100 BC) and to us (in 2100 AD).

We apply these promises to all people, but particularly to four groups of people in the United States.

Baby Boomers. (Born between 1946 and 1964) They are hard-working and professional. In younger years, they watched the same three TV networks day and night. Many of them are affluent and self-actualized. Yet Jesus said, "What do you benefit if you gain the whole world but lose your own soul? Is anything worth more than your soul?"

(Matthew 16:26) Jesus has a huge place for "boomers" in His plan of salvation if they will believe in Him. If they do, He will set them free.

Generation Xers. (1965 – 1976) They are diverse. They tend to be accepting, inclusive, technologically astute, and entrepreneurial. Many of their characteristics are those Jesus displayed. He loved diversity and included different types of people when He offered them His freedom and salvation. No one is more diverse or accepting than Jesus. "In this new life, it doesn't matter if you are a Jew or a Gentile, circumcised or uncircumcised, barbaric, uncivilized, slave, or free. Christ is all that matters and he lives in all of us." (Colossians 3:11) That unity includes Generation Xers. God offers to include them with all others who put their faith in Him. If they come to Him, He will set them free and give them His eternal life.

Millennials/Generation Y. (1977 – 1995) These men and women are noted for collaboration, transparency, balance in life, and instant gratification. They work hard and play hard. With their bent toward collaboration, they may find it easy to come to Jesus, because He collaborates with billions in building His Kingdom. They like transparency; Jesus is transparent to anyone who wants to know Him. They appreciate balance in their lives. Jesus sees life in perfect balance. They will enjoy God's perfect balance if they live as He intended. They want instant gratification. Jesus gives freedom the instant they believe in Him as their Savior and Lord. They understand hard work. Jesus worked hard. " . . . Because of the joy awaiting him, he endured the cross, disregarding its shame. Now he is seated in the place of honor beside God's throne." (Hebrews 12:2) He is calling millennials to sit with Him in heaven. They need to be transparent with Him. If they do, Jesus will set them free and give them His eternity.

Generation Z/iGeneration. (Mid 1990s – Present) They are Internet-savvy because they were born into the latest technological age. Due to growing up through the Great Recession they may have some unsettlement and insecurity.[36] They quickly and efficiently shift between work and play; they expect loyalty from business brands and retail companies; they love individuality. Nearly 92 percent of them have a digital footprint and they are globally minded. Above all, they are great at multi-tasking. " . . . they will create a document on their school computer, do research on their phone or tablet while taking notes on a notepad, then finish in front of the TV with a laptop, while face-timing a friend. You get the picture."[37]

Jesus enabled inventors to create the Internet and technology. It is in His timing that Generation Z was born into the technological age. If they are more conservative with their money due to bad experiences with the Great Recession, they are wiser than most because " . . . the love of money is the root of all kinds of evil." (1 Timothy 6:10) Use it wisely. They are probably the world's most awesome multitaskers. Jesus identifies with them as He multitasks globally, in the lives of billions of people, directly, technologically, and over the Internet. He never becomes tired. He destroyed the power of evil for them and offers them His gift of freedom from evil in this life and for eternity. Believe in Him and receive His free gift.

There is also good news for unbelievers. Believers are no better than you are. The only difference between believers and unbelievers is the main character in the Bible—Jesus. He said, " . . . He has sent me to proclaim freedom for the prisoners . . ." (Luke 4:18) When believers accepted Him, He gave them that freedom. Entertainment, movies, and television programs inundate our culture with evil. None of us need to be under any evil or mesmerized by it. Jesus will set anyone free who wants to be free. When we make that choice, we start to experience the gratification, peace, and freedom of living in God's presence. He offers this in good faith. Come and get it!

God calls out to all people from all ages and nations. If you come to Jesus so He can set you free, He will build His character traits into you. When you go to heaven you will take these traits with you into eternity.

CHAPTER 34

So What?
(Present date)

> "... I have appointed you as a watchman ... Whenever you receive a message from me, warn people immediately ... I will hold you responsible for their deaths ... If you warn them ... you will have saved yourself because you obeyed me." (Ezekiel 3:17-19)

SO WHAT? WHAT IS so important about the Bible's central message? What difference does it make?

Eternity hangs in the balance.

This book deals with the most critical issue in the history of this universe—restoring people to God. If there is one thing God is interested in, it is this: "I take no pleasure in the death of wicked people. I only want them to turn from their wicked ways so they can live. Turn! Turn from your wickedness." (Ezekiel 33:11)

Jesus put it in this positive tone, "So if the Son sets you free, you will be free indeed." (John 8:36 NIV)

Knowing what we know now makes all the difference in the world because we know God's heart. We started this book with Hosea 4:6, "My people are destroyed from lack of knowledge [about God]." We learned the human race was separated from God when the devil deceived Adam and Eve to rebel against Him in the Garden of Eden. Many yearn to know God but do not know how to get in touch with Him. To correct that tragedy, God sent Jesus to this world to defeat the devil and set people free. Jesus sets us free from powers greater than ourselves so we can know God.

Having learned the central message, we are better equipped to continue Jesus' Great Commission to tell the world about Him. He sends us into our cultures, to our families, friends, and acquaintances, to pull them out of the quicksand of spiritual imprisonment and death. The person who found a million bucks in grandpa's attic cannot help but tell others the good news. The good news is, believe in Jesus and He will restore you to God. You will know God who will help you in your problems. He will give you an abundant life with freedom in this life and the next. That answers the "So what?" question.

God urges us to proclaim the good news to others. Sometimes, we keep our mouths shut due to inability, embarrassment, awkwardness, or because we fear we might offend someone. God taught me a lesson through a believer in another country who had converted to Christianity.

He knew I was a believer and a guest in his country. His face was stern and his jaw was set as he said, "If we get caught by the religious police tonight, you will be sent back to your country but we [local believers] will be sent to jail and at noon on Friday we will be beheaded in the city square."

I was stunned. I never heard this from anyone who believed in Jesus. I never met a believer who was willing to die for his Christian faith. I was thousands of miles from home, in a desert, face-to-face with a man who stared death in the eye every day. His total submission to Jesus swept me off my feet. His spiritual strength made me envious. He followed Jesus without fear of rejection, embarrassment, or death.

What made that man so strong in his faith? He understood the Bible's central message that Jesus came to set him free from evil to restore him to God. He felt total freedom in his spirit as he defied death to its face.

I listened to him that evening as I leaned against the doorjamb between the kitchen and the living room. I needed that doorjamb to steady myself, because I was stunned by what he told me. I saw the look in his eyes; he would not give way to fear. That man was committed and willing to pay the ultimate price for his faith, if need be. I was convicted by his conviction. I felt the same resolute spirit come into me. I would never be the same again.

There are people who long for God and do not know Him. There are believers who love the Lord and want a deeper walk with Him. I have worked with many since I became a believer in Jesus fifty years ago. I have pulled "all-nighters" with military personnel and others who poured out their hearts, wanting a real, no-kidding relationship with God.

If you want a real relationship with God, I encourage you to find a place to be alone with God and ask Him to talk to you. Then be quiet. Listen. Tune your ear to God and you will hear Him. He will communicate with you in a thought, a nudge, an impression, idea, memory, urge, or whatever. Once you hear Him, you will experience an inner exhilaration with a peace that passes all understanding. (Philippians 4:7)

After that, look forward to the next time and yearn to hear God again. That will develop into a lifestyle and you will take moments during your busy schedule to hear God regularly. Remember what He tells you. Jot it down. Obey Him and do what He tells you to do. Then expect His explosive results. It is exhilarating! As long as we walk closely with our Lord, He will blitz our lives with His presence, peace, and power.

General Omar Bradley, one of the greatest generals in World War II, gave an alarming evaluation of the USA when he spoke on Armistice Day in 1948, "We have too many men of science, too few men of God.

We have grasped the mystery of the atom and rejected the Sermon on the Mount . . . Ours is a world of nuclear giants and ethical infants. We know more about war than we know about peace, more about killing than we know about living."[38]

That sounds like it could be said today, but General Bradley spoke those words almost seven decades ago. This world needs men and women who follow Jesus, who *live* the Sermon on the Mount, who *are* ethical giants, and who *know* the will and peace of God.

Too many professed Christians talk as if Jesus is real but live as if He is not. Remember the frog in a pot of water on a stovetop that slowly boils to death? At first, he is comfortable. The temperature slowly rises. The unassuming frog continues to sit in the water until it is too late. It is not too late for us. Together, we can know the redemptive message in the Bible and make that our priority, living and sharing it with others. We experience God's supernatural freedom and enjoy knowing Him! We want to tell others so they can also know Him.

A leading theologian, RC Sproul, gave his assessment of the modern American church, " . . . the organized church, the institutional church, is one of the most corrupt institutions in America, and in a way, is THE most corrupt; in light of the principle that 'to whom much is given, much is required,' and in light of the weight of the gifts Christ has given to the church and what we have done with those gifts, it is a scandal." [39]

Enough of the problem.

We have the solution! Christ lives in every true believer. (Colossians 1:27) "For God in all His fullness was pleased to live in Christ." (Colossians 1:19)

When Jesus comes to live in us by His Spirit, He brings all the fullness of God with Him and fills us with God. We are then complete. This means we have all of God's fullness in us. God sets us free to live right and equips us to go into the world to bring freedom to more people.

A plumber can show what Jesus is like to his friends. A CEO can treat his employees ethically. The Christian mother can nurture her children by the guidance of Holy Spirit; she can instruct them regarding what they may or may not watch on TV. The disciplined train engineer can honor the conductor. The Silicon Valley executive can honor God for the great strides in informational technology, and use that technology as he builds the Kingdom of God. The Christian counselor presents Jesus as she applies God's proven psychological insights to her clients. The list is endless.

"Those who are victorious will sit with me on my throne just as I was victorious and sat with my Father on his throne." (Revelation 3:21) Pull up a chair after your victories and sit with Jesus. He told that truth to the lukewarm church in the city of Laodicea and He is speaking the same promise of victory to the modern church in this twenty-first century.

Do you want to see how volatile the name of Jesus is? Include it in a discussion on terrorism, politics, LGBT, religious freedom, or any emotional topic. You will receive responses from anger to xenophobia.

We do not back away. We love people and want God to restore them from captivity so they can be set free from their prisons and know Him. Christianity is not always comfortable. It may be great to be in church and be blessed but at times God calls us to the brink of hell to help someone who wants God. I learned a saying that has helped me over the years. "Some people want to live next to a church with a ringing bell; I want to pitch my tent within a yard of hell."[40] Jesus calls believers to be victorious. We are victorious when we obey Him but it may not be easy.

I participated in war games with the marines while I was stationed at Kadena Air Base, Okinawa, Japan. Our conditions became worse as the wind increased and howled all night. Tents leaked and collapsed. The rain soaked every bit of clothing. The mud, grass, and weeds did not taste good as we slithered through them, doing the low crawl, scooping muck into our shirtsleeves every time we moved. Creeping, crawling critters found their way into our jacket necklines. Focusing on the commander and the mission helped me through. It is no different with Christianity. When believers focus on Jesus, we make it through tough times such as rejection, betrayal by a church, divorce, loss of a job, being broke, or hunger.

We win against evil even though a false gospel is spreading throughout the United States and the world. We have the same problem the Galatian church had in AD 49 when the apostle Paul wrote, "I am shocked that you are turning away so soon from God, who called you to himself through the loving mercy of Christ. You are following a different way that pretends to be the Good News but is not the Good News at all. You are being fooled by those who deliberately twist the truth concerning Christ." (Galatians 1:6-7)

Approximately twenty-one hundred years later, many in our secular society are twisting the gospel by teaching that all religions lead to God, or it does not matter what you believe if you are sincere. This teaching blocks God from our lives. He is not mentioned in the news or discussed in public. He is ignored; hence, biblical ignorance. Just what the devil wants?

God's answer: " . . . The God of our ancestors raised Jesus from the dead . . . put him in the place of honor at his right hand as Prince and Savior. He did this so . . . people . . . would repent of their sins and be forgiven." (Acts 5:29-32)

God's truth always comes back to the central message in the Bible: God sent Jesus to set humans free from evil so they could know God. No matter what losses we suffer in life, we need to focus on what is ultimately important—God sets us free so we can know Him.

The church wins the victory when she follows her Lord into battle. Seven times in Revelation (chapters 2 and 3), Jesus promised rewards to those who remain in Him and are victorious. He spoke to seven churches and gave each church the same message: victory.

To the church at **Ephesus:** " . . . To everyone who is victorious I will give fruit from the tree of life in the paradise of God." (Revelation 2:7)

To the church in **Smyrna:** " . . . whoever is victorious will not be harmed by the second death." (Revelation 2:11)

To the church in **Pergamum:** " . . . everyone who is victorious I will give to each one a white stone, and on the stone will be engraved a new name that no one understands except the one who receives it." (Revelation 2:17)

To the church in **Thyatira:** "To all who are victorious . . . I will give authority over all the nations." (Revelation 2:26, 29)

To the church in **Sardis:** "All who are victorious will be clothed in white. I will never erase their names from the Book of Life, but I will announce before my Father and his angels that they are mine." (Revelation 3:5, 6)

To the church in **Philadelphia:** "All who are victorious . . . I will also write on them my new name." (Revelation 3:12, 13)

To the church in **Laodicea:** "Those who are victorious will sit with me on my throne, just as I was victorious and sat with my Father on his throne." (Revelation 3:21, 22)

So what? Nothing is more important than freedom from evil so we can know God. Jesus the Messiah makes that possible.

CHAPTER 35

Now What?
(Present date)

"And how can they hear about him unless someone tells them?"
(Romans 10:14)

PUT YOUR SHOES ON and go into the world to bring the news that Jesus brought twenty-one hundred years ago. In biblical times, conquering armies removed the shoes or sandals from their prisoners as a sign of their captivity. When they released them, they returned their shoes. This practice made shoes a sign of release from captivity. God released believers from satan's captivity and gave us our shoes back. Let's use them as we go out to rescue others from the devil's grasp.

While the Israelites traveled through the desert from Egypt to the promised land, their shoes never wore out. "For all these forty years your clothes didn't wear out, and your feet didn't blister or swell . . . I led you through the wilderness, yet your clothes and sandals did not wear out . . . so you would know that he is the Lord your God." (Deuteronomy 8:4; 29:5, 6)

God freed His people from Egyptian captivity approximately 3,600 years ago. The fact that their sandals did not wear out on their journey was a sign of their freedom. Likewise, God freed us from lucifer's captivity. Our spiritual shoes will not wear out in our wilderness journey either, as long as we follow Him.

God created humans, land, oceans, air, and space. He wrapped every square inch of His creation in His love and power. By His power He defeats all that is wrong in our lives and lavishes us with His special agape, saving love in every area of our lives.

Picture yourself sitting with God in His throne room in heaven. He will destroy His archenemy and all evil powers once and for all. They will not be able to conquer us anymore. In Christ, we are more than conquerors over them. (Romans 8:37)

With this in mind, we participate with God in His agape love. As others experience the Creator's love and believe in Him, we become united with them. This unity among us is God's desire for humanity. All who call on Him will be saved and set free. When people come to faith in Jesus Christ and are baptized by Holy Spirit into the Body of Believers worldwide, they have true fellowship and unity with each other in Christ. Jesus prayed to His Father this would happen. "Just as you sent me into the world, I am sending them . . . I am praying not only for these [eleven] disciples but also for all who will believe in me through their message. I pray they will be one just as you and I are one . . ." (John 17:18-21)

Jesus sent His disciples into the world twenty-one hundred years ago. He sends His church in every generation to bring the Creator's genuine, life-changing enlightenment called freedom. The people of this modern world need to hear from God's people regarding His spiritual, front-page news that they may know nothing about.

Paul compared true believers with people who willfully continued to sin. He gave a list of those sins in 1 Corinthians 6:9-19, and then said, "Some of you [believers] *were* once like that. But you *were* cleansed, you *were* made holy; you *were* made right with God by calling on the name of the Lord Jesus Christ and by the Spirit of our God." (1 Corinthians 6:11)

Jesus set believers free from those and other sins. Sin does not have power over us anymore.

Now what? We tell our story about how God cleaned *us* up. That is the best place to start. We all know our own story best, and it is easier to tell because we experienced firsthand how God changed us. Therefore, your story may be the gospel presentation that changes someone's life. Let your life change start the life change in someone else.

God equips us to break into our secular culture, which is choking out the gospel from the public square. Os Guinness said, "We must discern and demolish its idols and repair its spreading damage. We must restore our own healthy practice of Christian tradition and renew its life-giving transmission that reflects the character of the Lord, who we worship."[41]

Think about the story of the prodigal son returning to his father (Luke 15). Many of our stories are similar to his. I rejected the love of God and went into the world of parties, hot cars, women, and booze. When I returned to God, my Father ran to meet me. Instead of first cleaning me up, He gave me a bear hug as He welcomed me back home. Our compassionate, heavenly Father runs up the road to meet each of us and gives us His bear hug. As He hugs us, He gets our pig slop on His clothes. While He smells the stench, He kisses us and welcomes us into His eternal family. This is agape love. This is God's love, by which He sets you and me free in our lives and eternity.

As you put your life-change story together, it may help to look at stories of others. Here are a few examples of how God changed lives within the last eighty years. Some names have been changed to protect privacy.

A Doolittle Raider led the commander of the Japanese attack on Pearl Harbor to Jesus Christ.

This is the incredible story of the lead pilot of the December 7, 1941, raid on Pearl Harbor. Fuchida was the one who shouted the war cry, "Tora, Tora, Tora!" Mitsuo Fuchida fought the United States throughout WWII and was intimately involved in the planning and leadership of the Japanese war effort as flight commander and later as a senior operations officer. After the war, Fuchida was a defeated warrior in occupied Japan, farming to meet the needs of his family. In 1950, Fuchida miraculously came to know Jesus Christ as Saviour through a tract [brochure] handed to him while exiting a train in Tokyo. The tract was entitled, "I Was a Prisoner of Japan," written by Jacob DeShazer who was one of the famous Doolittle Raiders. DeShazer trusted Christ as his Saviour while held captive by Japan for 40 months. DeShazer went to Japan in 1948 as a missionary and preached to the nation who held him captive [handing out the brochure that Fuchida received]. Fuchida faithfully served Jesus Christ as an evangelist until his death in 1976. "From Pearl Harbor to Calvary" is Fuchida's testimony of salvation.[42]

Jake DeShazer and Mitsuo Fuchida, once mortal enemies in WWII, met later and became close friends. Both became evangelists, preached Jesus Christ in Japan and the United States, and at times preached together. What an awesome example of how the Kingdom of God supersedes the kingdoms of man.

Spike, a member of my Bible class in San Antonio, Texas, confessed, "I've always wanted and asked for wrong things."

I asked him, "What are some wrong things you asked for?"

He said, "I wanted more money, better health, to get ahead in life, a better job. They were all, 'I want,' 'I want,' 'I want.' I was selfish."

"What are right things to ask for?"

"I want to know God better. I want to get closer to Him. I want to understand Him more and live in His presence."

Spike is doing that today. He used to be hooked on heroin, but not anymore. He *was* like that but now he is clean, made holy, and made right with God by calling on Jesus as Holy Spirit leads him.

Wilford Hall Medical Center (WHMC) was once the epicenter of medical care for the United States Air Force. After I arrived there on assignment, I met the commander. He told me he did prayer walks around the entire medical center campus, including parking lots and open areas. He said it all belonged to him because he was "the boss," so he decided that if he was responsible for everything that happened there, he wanted to make sure it was in God's hands. He dedicated the medical center to God as he walked around the property, praying for the Lord's protection, leadership, wisdom, and healing for all who entered and left WHMC. I joined him.

At one point, we teamed up and hosted a regional health conference on holistic medicine. The panel consisted of a medical doctor, psychologist, and chaplain. In the opening session, the doctor introduced himself: "Hello, I'm Doctor Smith, I'm your medical provider." The audience politely responded with a round of applause.

The psychologist introduced herself: "Hello, I'm Doctor Jones, I'm your psychological provider." Applause.

The chaplain introduced himself: "Hello, I'm Chaplain _____, I'm your spiritual provider." Stone silence.

I was that chaplain. The audience of medical professionals was used to having medical and psychological personnel as participants on a medical panel, but not a chaplain. In their way of thinking, the doctor and psychologist represented the body and soul of a person and that was enough.

That type of thinking is based on the secular belief that a human is made up of only the two aspects of body and soul, physical and psyche. However, the Bible says, "Now may the God of peace make you holy in every way, and may your whole spirit and soul and body be kept blameless until our Lord Jesus Christ comes again." (1 Thessalonians 5:23)

The Bible adds "spirit" to soul and body. God wants us wholly holy, completely holy. Without the spirit, the person is only two-thirds healed. The audience at our health conference functioned on two-thirds capacity, focusing only on the body and soul of their patients. They relegated the chaplain to private counseling, prayer, and chapel services, not public leadership, teaching, and training other professionals in spiritual issues. This is an example of how pastors, chaplains, and the church are relegated to the sidelines in our secular society.

Simply being on the panel as a chaplain was a challenge to the bias of some people. As a member of the panel, I gave examples of scientifically researched healings for the audience, in which faith and prayer were practiced alongside medical and psychological procedures. I gave evidence of how faith made a significant difference in the healing process. I also gave other examples of patients who practiced their faith in response to bad medical news and lived through tough and painful traumas with inner strength from God. The last example I gave was that of placing a chaplain next to the head of every trauma patient who came into the emergency room. Truly holistic medicine was a breakthrough as God's presence was brought into people's lives.

The next example happened at the conclusion of a retreat for high schoolers. One cold evening, hungry teens gathered around a roaring fire and enjoyed devouring smoking hot dogs, burnt marshmallows, and gooey s'mores. After the gourmet meal, the leader said that anyone who wanted to pray out loud was free to do so. Arty, a rough-mouthed youth who came to believe in Jesus during that weekend, prayed, "God, thanks for giving us a helluva good time."

No snickers, no muffled laughs. God had done spiritual surgery in many young lives and Arty was one of them. We welcomed him into

God's family. He cleaned up his language as he matured in his Christian faith.

At a European Christian men's conference, a man in his early thirties gave his life to Christ during the three-day meeting. In the car ride back home to Stuttgart, Germany, he told his friends, "I'm a changed man. Can't wait to get home to my wife so she can meet her new husband!"

The apostle Paul told his trainee, Timothy, "[in the last days people] ... will act religious but they will reject the power that could make them godly." (2 Timothy 3:5) I believe we are living in the end times. Stay obedient, do what God tells you to do, and you will see His power at work as He changes lives.

Each human who hears the good news about Jesus has to make a choice to follow or not to follow Him. When we believe in Jesus, God sets us free from our sins and calls us out from this world's systems. He gives His life and direction to us. Once He has restored us to God we no longer fit comfortably in our culture. We belong to God. Jesus came to transform culture and calls us to do the same. "The world would love you as one of its own if you belonged to it, but you are no longer part of the world. I chose you to come out of the world . . ." (John 15:19)

As followers of the Creator of the universe, our vision for eternal rescue must be wide enough, high enough, and deep enough to transform the enticing, disturbed, and explosive cultures of our modern world. Let's put our faith in God and rest in Him. We can take a lesson from the robin and the sparrow.

> "Said the robin to the sparrow,
> I should really like to know,
> Why these anxious human beings
> Rush about and worry so.
> Said the sparrow to the robin,

Friend I think that it must be,
That they have no heavenly Father
Such as cares for you and me."[43]

He cares for you and me so much that Jesus destroys the enemies who seek to keep us imprisoned. This is how God sums it up: " . . . Now he uses us to spread the knowledge of Christ everywhere . . . To those perishing, we are a dreadful smell of death and doom. But to those who are being saved, we are a life-giving perfume . . ." (2 Corinthians 2:14-16)

That life-giving perfume comes in the name, power, and authority of Jesus, who said, "The Spirit of the Lord is upon me, for he has anointed me to bring Good News to the poor. He has sent me to proclaim that captives will be released, that the blind will see, that the oppressed will be set free, and that the time of the Lord's favor has come." (Luke 4:18-19)

Nothing can completely prevent Jesus and His church from bringing the good news that captives will be released and the oppressed will be set free. He guarantees success for His mission. The Spirit of the Lord was upon Him and anointed Him to bring His good news to the world. The church relishes His success and joins Him in destroying evil and setting people free so they can know God.

The song "The Church Triumphant" with its interludes, captures that divine truth.

God has always had a people. Many a foolish conqueror has made the mistake of thinking that because he had forced the church of Jesus Christ out of site, he had stilled its voice and snuffed out its life, but God has always had a people . . . who cannot be bought, blabbered, murdered or stilled. On through the ages they march, the church! God's church triumphant!

Let the Church be the Church
Let the people rejoice

For we've settled the question
We've made our choice
Let the anthems ring out, songs of victory swell
For the church triumphant, is alive and well.

Listen child of God, it's alive . . . So, family of God, lift your hands, lift your hands and praise the Lord . . . God's church triumphant is alive, it's alive my friends. Alive and well.[44]

As God sent Queen Esther at the perfect time in history to save the Jewish nation in the Old Testament (Esther 4:14), so He sends His body of believers into this world "for such a time as this." May no one say about us, "Why did it take you so long to say something?" Instead, let us hear them say, "Thank you for coming and telling us about Jesus. He set us free. Now we know God."

Knowing God was Jesus' desire for believers. He said in a portion of His prayer to His Father, "And this is the way to have eternal life – to know you, the only true God, and Jesus Christ, the one you sent to earth." (John 17:3)

Appendix

THE VERSES LISTED BELOW are the central message in the Bible from beginning to end. They are the spine to the Bible, like the vertebrae in our backbones that contain the spinal cord from top to bottom. I list them as they appear in the Bible and this book. They show how God developed His plan to restore humans to Him in this life and eternity. The better we know and understand these scriptures in their proper order, the better we know God, understand the Bible, and apply God's freedom to ourselves.

Indented verses correspond directly with the scriptures listed above them as fulfilled prophecies.

CREATION
Genesis 1-2:25; God creates the universe.
Genesis 2:16-17; Prohibitive Command – God commands Adam not
　　to eat from one tree.
FALL
Genesis 3:1-14; Adam and Eve fall into sin.

REDEMPTION

Genesis 3:15; God promises restoration.

Genesis 12:1-3; God starts His plan to form the nation of Israel from Abram and Sarai.

Galatians 3:8; This verse has the same promise found in Genesis 12:3.

Genesis 15:1-6; God works His plan of salvation through Abraham's faith.

Genesis 17:1-7; God's promise goes global.

Romans 4:11; Abraham is the spiritual father of all who have faith.

Galatians 3:16; God gave His promises to Abraham and His seed [child] – Jesus the Christ.

Genesis 49:10; God chose the tribe of Judah to bring the Messiah into this world.

Exodus 3:1-14; God the "I AM" releases Israel from slavery.

John 8:31-59; Jesus is the "I AM."

2 Samuel 2:1-7; David is anointed king of Judah.

2 Samuel 7:16; God promises David that his kingdom will last forever. Jesus makes this true.

1 Kings 9:4-5; The Davidic kingdom continues through son Solomon and later Judean kings.

Luke 1:31-33; God gives Jesus the throne of his ancestor David, and He will reign forever.

1 Kings 8:41-43; 60-61; Israel's purpose was to show the world how great their God was.

Jeremiah 29:10-11; God has plans for a good future and hope for those who believe in Him.

Ephesians 1:9-10; All authority to carry out the above prophecy is given to Jesus.

John 3:16; Due to His authority, Jesus restores freedom to people around the world.

Daniel 2:31-45; God's Kingdom will crush all earthly kingdoms.

Revelation 11:15; Jesus came to build God's Kingdom

Micah 5:2; The Messiah will be born in Bethlehem of Judah.

Matthew 2:1; That prophecy is perfectly fulfilled.

1 Timothy 2:5-6; Jesus gives His life to purchase freedom for everyone.

Matthew 1:18; The Immaculate Conception: The Holy Spirit causes Mary to become pregnant.

Luke 2:1-20; The documented story of Jesus' birth into our world. The Messiah arrives.

Matthew 3:15-17; Jesus is baptized.

Matthew 4:1-11; The devil tempts Jesus to sin in the desert but Jesus defeats him.

Mark 1:15; Jesus begins His three-and-a-half-year ministry.

John 19:1-3; Jesus suffers for our sins.

Isaiah 53:5, 10; Isaiah prophesies the suffering.

John 19:18; Soldiers crucify Jesus.

John 19:30; Jesus dies.

John 19:41, 42; Joseph of Arimathea buries Jesus.

Matthew 28:5-6; Jesus rises from the dead.

Matthew 28:18-20; Jesus gives His Great Commission to His disciples.

Luke 24:50-52; Jesus ascends back into heaven.

Acts 1:8; On Pentecost Jesus baptized His church with His Holy Spirit.

Acts 2; On Pentecost, God the Holy Spirit comes to our world.

Acts 2:16-18; God pours out His Spirit on all people.

Joel 2:28-32; This prophecy was fulfilled.

Acts 15:8; God gives His Holy Spirit to Jewish and non-Jewish believers.

John 1:12; To all who receive Him, God gives the right to become His children.

Colossians 1:27; Through Holy Spirit, Jesus lives in every believer to work His plan.

Philippians 2:5; Believers have the mind of Christ; obey and continue the freedom plan.

Matthew 16:13-18; Jesus plans to build His church.

Ephesians 2:19-22; Jesus builds the cornerstone and foundation to His church.

1 Corinthians 12:13; Holy Spirit baptizes each new believer into the church.

1 Peter 2:5; Jesus builds believers throughout history into the super-structure of His church.

Ephesians 1:19-23; God gives supernatural power to His church for building His Kingdom.

Acts 9:1-20; Paul becomes the leader of the worldwide Christian church.

Ephesians 4:11-13; God gives the church spiritual gifts, enabling her for spiritual battle.

1 Corinthians 12-14; Holy Spirit equips His church for spiritual war.

Romans 12:6-8; Holy Spirit gives spiritual gifts to equip the church for her ministry.

1 Peter 4:10-11; Holy Spirit gives more spiritual gifts.

Galatians 5:22-23; Holy Spirit grows spiritual fruit in His church as her members mature.

Ephesians 6:13-17; Holy Spirit protects her with His spiritual armament.

Ephesians 6:18; Holy Spirit gives us the offensive weapon of prayer.

Matthew 6:17-18; The offensive weapon of fasting is given.

Revelation 1:5; The offensive weapon of Jesus' blood is given.

Luke 10:18-19; Jesus gives His authority over the power of the enemy, to the church.

2 Corinthians 10:3-5; The church doesn't fight people first, it fights spiritual forces.

1 Thessalonians 4:16-18; Jesus comes back to this world and saves His people.

Revelation 19:11-21; Jesus destroys His enemies: the Battle of Armageddon.

Revelation 20:7-10; Jesus destroys the last enemy left standing—the devil.

Revelation 20:11-15; God brings perfect justice on Judgment Day.

1 Corinthians 15:24-28; Jesus turns the Kingdom of God over to His Father.

Revelation 21:1-7; God creates the new heaven and earth, His perfect home for believers.

Revelation 21:6; God completes His plan when He says, "It is finished."

Revelation 22:16; Jesus confirms the Bible's central message that He is its one main character.

Revelation 7:9-10; We are home in heaven.

Notes

1   Barna, George. Charisma, July 2017, P. 18.

2   Keil & Delitzsch. Commentaries on the Old Testament: Ecclesiastes, WM. B.Eerdmans Publishing Co., Grand Rapids, MI, 1971, P. 261.

3   Grady, J. Lee. Charisma, February 2016, P. 66.

4   Guinness, Os. Impossible People, InterVarsity Press, Downers Grove, IL, 2016, P. 198.

5   Bewes, Richard. Decision Magazine, BGEA, Charlotte, NC, May 2016, P. 36.

6   The Celebration Hymnal, Word Music/Integrity Music, 1997.

7   www.biblegateway.com/scripture-engagement

8   Smith, Malcolm. This Son of Mine, Xulon Press, www.xulonpress. com, 2015, P. 78.

9   http://www.lyricsmode.com/lyrics/b/bill_gaither/let_freedome_ ring.html

10 Keil & Delitzsch. Commentaries on the Old Testament: The Pentateuch, Vol. 1. WM. B. Eerdmans Publishing Co., Grand Rapids, MI, 1971, P. 100.

11 www.hebrew-streams.org/frontstuff/jesus-yeshua.html

12 Rakes, Mike. www.charismamag.com, August 2015, P. 88.

13 www.anointedlinks.com/one_solitary_life.html

14 Holy Bible, New Living Translation, Tyndale House Publishers, Inc., Carol Stream, IL, 2007, P. 904.

15 www.biblestudytools.com/dictionary/goel

16 The Celebration Hymnal, Word Music/Integrity Music, 1997, P. 517.

17 Smith. This Son of Mine, Ibid. P. 14.

18 Ibid.

19 LeStrange, Ryan. Charisma, November 2016, P. 52 - 53.

20 www.tasc-creationscience.org/content/racism-human-races-or-one-blood

21 www.Gracefellowshipinternational.com

22 www.fishingtheabyss.com/archives/44

23 Twitter.com/mig4jc/status/733694438992646

24 Wallnau, Lance. Charisma Magazine, October 2016, P. 36.

25 Loveless, Bill. "A" Life? Or "THE" Life?. www.christislifeministries.com, P. 18.

26 http://mintools.com/gifts-list.htm

27 Smith, Malcolm. Turn Your Back on The Problem, Logos International, NJ, 1972, P. 54.

28 Ibid. P. 51.

29 www.JourneywithJesus.net/poemsandprayers/Teresa_of_Avila_Christ_Has_No_Body.shtml

30 www.pewforum.org

31 Yohanan, K.P. Revolution in World Missions, Gospel for Asia, Carrollton, TX, 2004, P. 133.

32 Psalter Hymnal, CRC Publications, Grand Rapids, MI, 1987, P. 861.

33 Garrison, David. A Wind in the house of Islam, WIGTake Resources, Monument, CO, 2014, P. 230.

34 www.Biblestudy.org/bibleref/meaning-of-numbers-in-the-bible/7. html

35 Words by C. Herbert Woolston, 1856 – 1927; Music by George F. Root, 1820 – 1895; copyright unknown.

36 En.wikipedia.org/wiki/Generation_Z

37 www.huffingtonpost. com/george-beall/8-key-differences-between_b_12814200.html

38 Bradley, General Omar N. Christianity Today, March 4, 1988, P. 30.

39 Sproul, R.C. 2006 Ligonier National Conference, "Bought with A Price."

40 Quote from C.T. Studd, goodreads.org.

41 Guinness, loc. Cit., P. 192.

42 www.biblebelievers.com/fuchida1.html

43 www.goodreads.com/quotes/714001/the-robin-and-the-sparrow

44 http://genius.com/Gaither-vocal-band-the-church-triumphant-lyrics

Order Information

REDEMPTION
P R E S S

To order additional copies of this book, please visit
www.redemption-press.com.
Also available on Amazon.com and BarnesandNoble.com
Or by calling toll free 1-844-2REDEEM.